AUTHORITY AND ORDER

The important questions in ecumenical dialogue centre upon issues of authority and order. This book uses the development of ministry in the early Methodist Church to explore the origins of the Methodist order and identify the nature of authority exercised by John Wesley, the founder of the Methodist Church.

Showing Methodism as having been founded upon Episcopalian principles, but in a manner reinterpreted by its founder, Adrian Burdon charts the journey made by John Wesley and his people towards the ordination of preachers, which became such a major issue amongst the first Methodist Societies. Implications for understanding the nature and practice of authority and order in modern Methodism are explored, with particular reference to the covenant for unity between English Methodists and the Church of England.

Authority and Order

John Wesley and his Preachers

ADRIAN BURDON
Methodist Minister, Leeds

Routledge
Taylor & Francis Group

LONDON AND NEW YORK

First published 2005 by Ashgate Publishing

Published 2016 by Routledge
2 Park Square, Milton Park, Abingdon, Oxon OX14 4RN
711 Third Avenue, New York, NY 10017, USA

Routledge is an imprint of the Taylor & Francis Group, an informa business

British Library Cataloguing in Publication Data
Burdon Adrian, 1962–
    Authority and Order: John Wesley and his Preachers.
    1. Wesley, John, 1703–1791. 2. Methodist Church – History – 18th century.
    3. Church – Authority. I. Title
    262.8

US Library of Congress Cataloging in Publication Data
Burdon Adrian, 1962–
    Authority and Order: John Wesley and his Preachers / Adrian Burdon.
    p. cm.
    Includes bibliographical references and index.
    1. Methodist Church – Government. 2. Church – Authority. 3. Wesley, John,
    1703–1791. I. Title.
    BX8340.B87 2006
    262'07–dc22   2005011773

ISBN 9780754654544 (hbk)

Contents

Acknowledgements

Debts are, on the whole, commonly regarded as disagreeable things. In the present setting, however, there are a number of debts with which I am more than happy to live. It is with gratitude that I acknowledge my debt to those who have encouraged me in the pursuit of Methodist and Liturgical interests. All students and scholars depend for their development upon the encouragement of those who have gone before them. For the nurturing and development of my interest in matters liturgical I am indebted to the Rev Dr Richard Buxton and the Rt Rev Dr Kenneth W. Stevenson, friends and tutors. Richard has been continuously generous and gracious in supervision of my undergraduate studies, as well as later Master's and Doctoral theses. For my interest in Methodist history, I remain indebted to the Rev Dr Henry Rack, former Bishop Fraser Senior Lecturer in Ecclesiastical History at the University of Manchester. In bringing these two areas of interest together, I shall be forever grateful for the kindness and encouragement of the late Revs A. Raymond George and Gordon S Wakefield. They are, truly, friends on earth and friends above.

Introduction

On 1 November 2003 the Methodist Church in Britain and the Church of England entered into a Covenant which bound them together to work towards full and visible unity. This relationship establishes the two Churches as fellow travellers, committed to overcoming the obstacles that have impeded previous schemes for unity. These impediments have centred largely upon issues of ministry, particularly ordained ministry, and upon the expression and exercise of authority. The popular caricature, which is never far from the truth, suggests that the Church of England must overcome remaining difficulties about the ministry of women, and the Methodist Church must give serious consideration to the incorporation of the historic episcopate into its structure.

In January 2005 the General Synod of the Church of England made a decision which paved the way towards the removal of the legal processes that prevent the consecration of women bishops. A report was put to the Methodist Conference, meeting at Torquay, in June 2005, which outlined the various ways episcopacy might be incorporated into the Methodist structure. Parallel papers led the Conference in consideration of the structure of ministry and the nature of authority within the Methodist Church.[1]

Connexionalism, the structure which enables the interdependence of local Churches and people in relation to the annual Conference, is an important concept for the Methodist way of being Church. Episcopacy is exercised corporately through the various elements of Circuit, District and Conference. This is an expression of episcopacy in which governance, management and leadership are enabled and by which all people, including those exercising the oversight, are watched over in love.[2]

The Methodist Church has a distinctive history and the development of ordained ministry has a significant part in that history. Today's Presbyters trace the origins of their office to that of the Assistants appointed by John Wesley to minister under his authority. The ministry of the Assistants was related to the ministry of John Wesley himself – their authority depended upon a continued

---

1   Papers, jointly presented by the Methodist Council and the Faith and Order Committee, addressed questions concerning *The Nature of Oversight*, *What is a Circuit Superintendent?* and *What Sort of Bishops?*. The full text of these papers is published in *The Agenda of the Methodist Conference* (Peterborough: Methodist Publishing House, 2005).

2   For a fuller consideration of the nature of Connexionalism and the nature of oversight in the Methodist Church, see *The Agenda of the Methodist Conference* (Peterborough: Methodist Publishing House, 2005).

relationship with the founder of the movement. In the modern Methodist Church, the authority of the Presbyters' ministry depends upon their being in connexion with the Methodist Conference. John Wesley's understanding and expression of authority, and his keeping of order amongst the early Methodists, are important topics. A study of the developing theme enables a glimpse into the lives of the people called Methodist. An aspect of the ethos of the Societies is revealed by the manner in which they were subject to John Wesley's authority. He was the founder of the Methodist movement and regarded himself as its scriptural episcopos.

John Wesley's exercise of authority can be seen particularly in his concern for the Methodist Societies to remain within the Church of England. An important issue was the question of the provision for sacramental ministry amongst the Societies. John Wesley believed that the only acceptable means of authorising his preachers for sacramental ministry would be ordination by prayer and the imposition of hands.

This work, which is divided into eight chapters with Prologue and Epilogue, centres upon the issue of the ministry of the Methodist preachers in order to identify the manner of John Wesley's authority. It traces the developing expression of Wesley's authority and his control of those who joined him in the Methodist Societies. The Prologue acknowledges that Wesley never intended to create a Church separate from the Church of England and never acknowledged that he had stepped beyond the bounds of that Church. Indeed, Chapter 1 recognises that Wesley set out on his ministry as a rigid establishment man obligated, and faithful, to the rubrics and canons of the Church of England. Chapter 2 observes that, following his 'conversion' experience, Wesley more and more stretched the word of those rubrics and canons in the favour of the spirit of evangelism. Chapter 3 of this work exemplifies such a stretching, charting the rise and development of the Assistants appointed by Wesley to help him in his work. It is important to acknowledge, though, that the ministry of these Assistants is exercised in relationship with John Wesley. The founder of the Methodist movement held his people in a rigid grip of control and, as is explored in Chapter 4, based his assertion of episcopacy on historical precedents.

It is inevitable that one must question the legitimacy of John Wesley's position. The reality was that, as a priest in the Church of England, he was not in the lawful position of being able to exercise the sort of authority that he claimed. Chapter 5 explores the legitimacy of Wesley's claim never to have separated from the Church, and questions whether his actions did indeed take him outside the boundaries of communion with it. The events which led up to Wesley ordaining his preachers are examined and the reactions of those around him, especially his brother Charles, recorded. Chapter 6 sees John Wesley reflecting upon his actions and gives attention to his sermon on the subject, *Prophets and Priests*, produced during his visit to Ireland in 1789. He continued to assert that ordination by prayer and the imposition of hands was the only right manner of authorising his preachers for a sacramental ministry. The sermon demonstrates Wesley asserting himself, its purpose being not apologetic but didactic. He was not intending to explain his actions, but to remind those associated with him how he expected them to respond to his authority. Chapters 7 and 8 relate to John Wesley's ordination of his preachers. They contain a commentary upon the ordinal used and show the text of that ordinal in parallel with the Prayer Book ordinal contemporary to Wesley's abridgment. To conclude, the Epilogue brings us back to the point that no matter how things developed, John Wesley never did formally leave the Church of England and never did intend that the Methodist people should separate from it. He used his understanding of having received both an ordinary and an extra–ordinary calling to justify his actions. His ordinary calling was to be a priest in the Church of England and his extra–ordinary calling was to do the work of an evangelist amongst those not yet touched by that Church. He believed himself to be setting the Church a good example for what he believed the whole people of God should be doing. His purpose had never been to found a new Church, but to raise up scriptural holiness in the land and to enliven the Church of England. The furtherance of both was his motivation for establishing his band of extraordinary messengers.

Over the past three centuries the tidal relationship between the Church of England and the people called Methodist has ebbed and flowed. The present Covenantal position is a sign of hope for a future visible organic union. This unity shall not, though, be created by Methodism returning to the Church but by both coming together as equal partners in something new and distinctive. There is much common history and it must be acknowledged that, whilst much of it brings the two bodies together, there are some parts of it which might also keep them apart. The expressions and practices relating to ministry and the place of authority contain aspects which fall into both categories. The relationship must move forward in penitence and faith in the spirit of reconciliation and humility.

Prologue

'I am a Church of England Man'

John Wesley had not the slightest intention of founding a new Church, but claimed, always, to be a faithful member and priest of the Church of England. He stated that, unless he was expelled, he would live and die in the fellowship of that Church.[1] Wesley never acknowledged the possibility that, by his actions, he had stepped beyond her fellowship. Although admitting that he was sometimes 'at variance' with the Church, he never regarded himself as being in schism.

Wesley's contemporaries, seeing his irregularities as movement away from the Church of England, were not convinced by his claims of fidelity. His statements and actions made the faithful band of evangelical clergymen, who had gathered around him, feel nervous. Along with his brother, Charles Wesley, men like Grimshaw of Haworth, Fletcher of Madeley, Venn of Huddersfield, and Walker of Truro, exerted a calming influence upon the otherwise impetuous John Wesley. They pointed out that, if he went too far in his 'variance' from the Church, he would find himself without their support.[2]

Despite his claims then, John Wesley's actions were interpreted as taking him out of the Church of England; nor was it only his contemporaries who made such assessments. Dr Joseph Beaumont, a popular nineteenth-century Wesleyan preacher said, at the 1834 Wesleyan Conference, that John Wesley had, 'like a good oarsman, looked one way and rowed another.'[3]

John Wesley did, though, make a great effort to keep the Methodist Societies within the fellowship of the Church of England. One of the intentions for the Societies was to encourage spiritual growth within the Church. John Wesley did not envisage that the members of those Societies would seek separation from the Church of England. When it became apparent that the Methodists wanted to separate from the Church, Wesley used his authority, as founder of the movement, to discourage his people from taking that step.

---

1   John Telford (ed.), *The Letters of the Rev John Wesley, A.M.*, 8 vols (London: Epworth, 1931), 8:58. 6 May 1788 to Henry Moore: 'I am a Church-of-England man; and … in the Church I will live and die, unless I am thrust out.'

2   An example of this happening can be seen in the correspondence between Grimshaw of Haworth and Charles Wesley regarding the preachers at Norwich administering the sacraments in 1760. See below, page 51.

3   Benjamin Gregory, *Sidelights on the Conflicts of Methodism, 1827–52.* (London: Caswell, 1899), 161. Dr Joseph Beaumont (1794–1855) had the reputation of being liberal in his views. He was often found opposing Jabez Bunting.

John Wesley realised that the single-most important factor in preventing, or promoting, the movement of Methodists away from the Church of England, concerned the question of sacramental ministry. Some of his people, feeling the Anglican clergy to be unworthy, wanted to receive Holy Communion from the hands of the Methodist Preachers. The issue became of increased importance in those places where the parish clergy refused to allow the Methodists admission to the sacrament. Wesley, however, for most of his life, believed that the authorisation of his Preachers to administer the sacraments would lead to the separation of the Methodists from the Church of England. This was a step that he was not willing to countenance.

John Wesley demanded total obedience from his people, and exerted absolute authority over them. He exercised an expression of authority in which there was no room for appeal. His was the authority of the founder of a movement keeping control over those who chose to join him. If some disagreed with Wesley's ways, then they were always free to leave his company.

This was not the authority of a despot; it was, rather, the authority of one who felt himself under an extraordinary calling.[4] John Wesley was an evangelist, charged with the salvation of countless souls who, but for his faithfulness, would be forever damned. He was the Christian who believed his own salvation dependent upon fidelity to his calling. Wesley's understanding was expressed in the hymn written by his brother Charles, paraphrasing Matthew Henry's *Commentary* on Leviticus 8:31-6:[5]

A charge to keep I have,
A God to glorify,
A never-dying soul to save,
And fit it for the sky;
To serve the present age,
My calling to fulfil,
O may it all my powers engage,
To do my master's will!

---

4   John Wesley's understanding of himself having both an ordinary and an extraordinary calling was outlined in his letter to his brother Charles Wesley, 23 June 1739, Telford *Letters*, 1 and Frank Baker, (ed.), *Letters* 1 (1721–39) in *The Works of John Wesley*, (Oxford: Clarendon, 1980), 25:660 and is discussed below, page 13f.

5   Matthew Henry's *Commentary* reads: 'We have every one of us a charge to keep, an eternal God to glorify, an immortal soul to provide for, needful duty to be done, our generation to serve; and it must be our daily care to keep this charge, for it is the charge of the Lord our Master, who will shortly call us to an account about it, and is at our peril if we neglect it. Keep it 'that ye die not'; it is death, eternal death, to betray the truth we are charged with.' For a further discussion see Franz Hilderbrandt and Oliver A. Beckerlegge (eds), *A Collection of Hymns for the Use of the People Called Methodists* in *The Works of John Wesley*, (Nashville: Abingdon, 1983), 7:465.

Arm me with jealous care,
As in thy sight to live;
And Oh! thy servant, Lord, prepare
A strict account to give.
Help me to watch and pray,
And on thyself rely,
Assured, if I my trust betray,
I shall for ever die.[6]

John Wesley was, then, a man motivated by the urgency of the evangelist. He felt himself uniquely charged, not only with the reaching after his own salvation, but also with the awakening of sleeping sinners who, otherwise, would die in the darkness of ignorance. Wesley's belief that all people could be saved, by grace through faith, was to become the primary premise to which all else must yield. This understanding found expression in the development of the Methodist Societies.

So effective was John Wesley's evangelical ministry that it became necessary for him to appoint Assistants to support him in his work. The progression of John Wesley's ideas about, and understanding of, the exercise of authority, went hand-in-hand with the development of the ministry of his Assistants. Wesley's pronouncements on the ministry of those associated with him must be seen in the context of his exercising authority as founder, and scriptural episcopos, of the people called Methodists.[7]

Wesley's ultimate test of truth was the test of fruits; good fruit coming only from good developments. It was this approach that would serve him well when dealing with Thomas Maxfield's taking up preaching. On that occasion, through his mother's influence, Wesley came to see that Maxfield was called of God to be a preacher.[8] It was, though, the same approach that caused him to be so rigid on the question of his preachers taking up a sacramental ministry. Wesley believed that the fruit of such a development would be the putting of the Methodist Societies beyond the fellowship of the Church of England. This, he believed, would be a bad fruit.

Whilst all his actions gave contrary signals, John Wesley continued to maintain his claim of loyalty to the Church of England, almost to the point of it becoming the fixation of a psychotic. John Wesley's insistence on claiming fidelity to the Church of England was a matter of great importance. He was concerned that his preachers should take no initiative that would lead them outside the fellowship of the Church. Wesley expected his associates to remain in the work to which he, the scriptural episcopos of the Methodist people, had appointed them.

---

6   Franz Hilderbrandt and Oliver A. Beckerlegge (eds) *A Collection of Hymns for the Use of the People Called Methodists*, item numbered 309.

7   The term 'scriptural episcopos' was used by John Wesley in his letter to his brother Charles Wesley, 19 August 1785. Telford, *Letters*, 7:284. 'I firmly believe I am a scriptural episcopos as much as any man in England or Europe ...'.

8   See below, page 23ff.

So it is that the study of Wesley's use of authority must be set within the context of the ministry of his preachers. It was within this context that Wesley's understanding of the nature of authority was given clear expression.

Chapter 1

Wesley's Initial Position
Authority of Rubric and Canon

John Wesley's understanding of the function of authority did not change during his life. He maintained that authority was to be exercised rigorously, without impartiality. Nor did Wesley's understanding of the source of authority undergo change; he understood authority as being from God. However, the way in which Wesley understood that authority to be communicated underwent significant change.

Before his momentous 'heart-warming' experience at Aldersgate Street, on 24 May 1738,[1] John Wesley's understanding of authority and order fell within the theological bounds of the eighteenth-century Church of England. He believed that authority was to be exercised according to the principles found in the rubrics of the *Book of Common Prayer (1662)*, and in the canons and Thirty-nine Articles of the Church of England. It was, partly, due to his rigid application of these views that Wesley had got into trouble whilst a missionary in Georgia. In his practice in the colony, the flexibility of the pastor was compromised by faithful, but rigid, application of rubric and canon.

In Georgia, John Wesley had become entangled in a love affair with Sophy Hopkey, the ward of Thomas Couston, the Chief Magistrate in the colony. He had met Sophy as she was recovering from a bad relationship, and found himself drawn into a romantic relationship with her. On 14 February 1787 Wesley informed Sophy of his belief that it was not right for them to marry.[2] The young girl, who had convinced herself that a proposal of marriage, if not already implied, was imminent, appeared to be distraught at his decision. Although subsequently marrying Mr Williamson, the bitter taste of rejection stayed with Sophy; her relationship with John Wesley remaining strained. Sophy exasperated the situation by encouraging the people of the colony to believe that she had been treated badly by Wesley.

Unfortunately, the next thing that happened was that Sophy fell foul of John Wesley's decision to apply the Prayer Book regulations in the colony. He

---

1   See the entry for 24 May 1738 in Nehemiah Curnock (ed.), *The Journal of the Rev. John Wesley, A.M.,* 8 vols, (London: Robert Culley, 1909—16), 1:472—77 and W. Reginald Ward and Richard P. Heitzenrater (eds), *Journals and Diaries: I (1735–38)* in *The Works of John Wesley*, (Nashville: Abingdon, 1988), 18:242–250.

2   W. Reginald Ward and Richard P. Heitzenrater (eds), *Journals and Diaries,* 18:472.

encouraged the people to adopt the rigorous spiritual exercises that he had enjoyed as a member of the Holy Club at Oxford. He required them to practise prayer and fasting, to be regular attenders at Morning Prayer, and to give notice of their intention to present themselves for communion. On 7 August 1737, Wesley sent Sophy away from the communion service because of her apparent bad conduct, and her failure to give notice of her intention to be present at the altar. This action put flame to the dry kindling of the already difficult relationship that existed between John Wesley and the people, leading to his having to flee the colony on 22 December 1737.[3]

Although John Wesley's ministry in Georgia had not been a great success, the period was, nevertheless, one of significance for his spiritual and intellectual development. It was during this time that, under the influence of the Moravians, Wesley came to revise some of his ideas concerning the ancient Church. His views had been largely formed through the combination of a number of rather conservative influences, including his father, the Oxford scholars, and the Manchester nonjurors.[4]

In September 1736 Wesley had, in the company of the Germans, followed a study of early Christian texts. He came to realise that, contrary to his previous opinion, the ancient documents and apostolic canons did not express the consensus of the early Christians. Wesley recognised some errors in his previous views of Christian antiquity. Consequently, he committed himself only to use antiquity to supplement the authority of scripture.[5]

John Wesley did, nonetheless, continue to turn to antiquity to strengthen the expression of his understanding. Even during his journey home from Georgia, in January 1738, he could be found appealing to Christian antiquity as a source of understanding for the church. Wesley recorded in his *Journal* that God had thrown him upon reading the works of Cyprian, the third century bishop of Carthage.[6] He wrote of having been impressed by Cyprian's presentation of episcopacy as the

---

3   Wesley tended to keep comment concerning this matter to a minimum in his *Journal*; most references are to be found in the *Diary* which runs parallel to the published *Journals*. Curnock *Journal*, 1:181–376. W. Reginald Ward and Richard P. Heitzenrater (eds), *Journals and Diaries*, 18:187–571. Further assessment of this story can be found in a number of standard biographies of John Wesley. A particularly useful account is given in Henry Rack, *Reasonable Enthusiast*, (London: Epworth, 1989), 124–36.

4   The Manchester nonjurors were a group of scholars, including Thomas Deacon and John Byrom, who tried to focus their faith upon the life and thought of the early Church. Wesley came into contact with their teaching through John Clayton who was leader of a religious society at Brasenose College which mirrored Wesley's own Holy Club. The coincidence of the influences of the Manchester nonjurors, John Wesley's father and the Oxford scholars is discussed in Ted A. Campbell, *John Wesley and Christian Antiquity*, (Nashville: Kingswood, 1991), 23–53.

5   See the entry for 13 September 1736 in W. Reginald Ward and Richard P. Heitzenrater, *Journals and Diaries*, 18:171.

6   Curnock, *Journal*, 1:416.

channel through which grace is conveyed to the church. Cyprian's scheme outlined that the Holy Spirit was given by Christ to the apostles, by the apostles to the bishops whom they ordained, and by those bishops to their successors. Thus, John Wesley, following Cyprian's reasoning, believed that an unbroken episcopal succession was necessary to give efficacy to all religious exercises.

Wesley's view on episcopacy, on the authority of the bishop, and on the church was, at this point, the contemporary expression of the Church of England. He would have endorsed wholeheartedly Cyprian's classic comment that 'hence you should know that the bishop is in the Church and the Church in the bishop, and if any one be not with the bishop he is not in the church.'[7] In this early period in his ministry, Wesley applied Cyprian's maxim to the Church of England and her bishops.

John Wesley's understanding of the nature and expression of authority in the church, at the beginning of 1738, showed him to be the stiff establishment clergyman typical of his era. Albert Outler has suggested that Wesley's understanding of the nature of the church finds its origins in the teachings of sixteenth–century English reformers, such as Thomas Cranmer, John Jewell and Richard Hooker.[8] Wesley's disciplinary practices in Georgia seem to have been particularly influenced by the pattern suggested by Jewell, whose words, in turn, reflect Christ's to St Peter. Jewell, suggesting the ministerial office might include the removal from, as well as the admission of members to, the church, wrote:

> we say that Christ hath given to his ministers power to bind, to loose, to open, to shut; … Out of doubt, what sentence soever the minister of God shall give in this sort, God himself doth so well allow of it that whatsoever here in earth by their means is loosed and bound God himself will loose and bind the same in heaven.[9]

John Wesley's attitude was exemplified by his practice in Georgia. He displayed a belief that the work of the pastor did include the exercising of authority and the keeping of order. Pastoral considerations were directed by the demands of authority and order. Despite the developments in John Wesley's understanding of ancient Christianity, he did not, yet, review his interpretation of the expression of authority. That his approach in Georgia might have been too rigorous, and, consequently, pastorally damaging, seemed not to enter into his thought. His reflections upon the experience seemed to lead him to the contrary decision. The traditional Church of England expression of authority was seen, by Wesley, as the

---

7   Cyprian, Ep.lxvi.7 quoted from Henry Bettenson (ed.), *Documents of the Christian Church*, (Oxford: OUP, Second Edition 1963), 74.

8   Albert C. Outler, *John Wesley*, (Oxford: OUP, 1964), 306. Thomas Cranmer (1489–1556), Archbishop of Canterbury; John Jewell (1552–1571), Bishop of Salisbury; Richard Hooker (1554—1600), Anglican Divine.

9   John Jewell, *An Apology of the Church of England*, 1564. Quoted from G.R. Evans and J. Robert Wright (eds), *The Anglican Tradition* (London: SPCK/Minneapolis: Fortress, 1991), 147–8. (cf. Matthew 16:18–19).

only acceptable option. This position would be one from which Wesley would never quite escape, although it would be modified by the change in expression. In early 1738, though, the demands of good order and discipline were equated with obedience to rubric and canon.

Chapter 2

After Aldersgate
Authority of a Warm-Hearted Evangelist

John Wesley's withdrawal from his work in Georgia was precipitated by, and advanced further, crises, both personal and spiritual. The period concluded with what became, for Wesley, the epoch-making experience at the meeting at Aldersgate Street on 24 May 1738. There is no evidence to suggest that the experience caused any change in Wesley's theology of ministry. The renewed vigour and evangelistic zeal with which he subsequently sought to convert the world, however, became the motivating force behind many an unusual development. John Wesley wrote to his brother Charles, on 23 June 1739:

> I have both an ordinary call and an extraordinary. My ordinary call is my ordination by the bishop ... My extraordinary call is witnessed by the works God doth by my ministry.[1]

Albert Outler has suggested that John Wesley understood his having been called to an 'extraordinary' ministry to help remedy the insufficiencies of the 'ordinary' ministry of the Church of England. 'This', wrote Outler, 'made him something rather like the superior-general of an evangelical order within a regional division of the Church catholic.'[2]

John Wesley's sense of special calling sustained him throughout his career of evangelism. 'It was', wrote Thompson, 'a conviction which was invincible. No opposition and no danger could shake it. It never failed, even in hours of darkness and seasons of spiritual aridity.'[3]

Wesley believed that the demands of his calling required him to go to those who needed him most, whether they were technically within his jurisdiction or not. At first he found that a number of clergymen invited him to speak from their pulpits, perhaps expecting the usual stories from a returned missionary. It soon became clear, though, that Wesley's message was unsettling, both to clergy and congregations, and pulpits began to be closed against him.

As more and more clergymen closed their Churches to John Wesley, so it became increasingly difficult for him to proclaim the message with which he felt

---

1   Telford, *Letters*, 1 and Baker, *Letters*, 25:660.
2   Albert C. Outler, *John Wesley*, 306.
3   Edgar W. Thompson, *Wesley: Apostolic Man, Some Reflections on Wesley's Consecration of Dr. Thomas Coke,* (London: Epworth, 1957), 60.

burdened. To the still conventional Churchman, the idea of preaching outside the Church building was his *bête noire*. According to the Church of England canons of 1604, the practice of preaching outside one's own appointed place, without the invitation of the incumbent clergyman or Church warden, was illegal. Furthermore, the Conventicle Act of 1670 declared preaching outside Church buildings to be illegal. Wesley would not, yet, easily challenge the authority of law with the demands of his evangelical calling.

That John Wesley did, in 1739, take up open-air field-preaching was due to the influence of George Whitefield, a former member of the Oxford Holy Club.[4] Whitefield had the reputation of being a great preacher and an effective evangelist. Downey has identified him as being gifted with an extraordinarily powerful voice. He had immense projection, rare tone, and a vast range with which to express every human emotion.[5] Whitefield believed that it was the duty of preachers to use every homiletic and oratorical device at their disposal to save people from hell.

There was much common ground between John Wesley and George Whitefield. They had both experienced a dynamic religious 'conversion' that had led to a passion to spread the Gospel. They shared scorn for the dryness of spirituality being offered by the Church of England. They were united in the desire to alleviate social injustice.

There were, though, many differences between the pair. Whilst Wesley was the scholar, Whitefield was the actor. Wesley's success was despite his gifts as a preacher, Whitefield's because of them. Wesley is remembered as the shrewd thinker, organiser and teacher; memory of Whitefield recalls only the supremely fine orator. Heitzenrater has commented that:

> If Wesley's stature as a theologian has been underestimated, his reputation as a preacher has probably been overestimated. Wesley's primary skill was not in the techniques of preaching; he certainly did not have the homiletical flair of a Whitefield.[6]

John Wesley's relationship with George Whitefield did not pass without contemporary comment. John's younger brother, Samuel, who considered Whitefield a fanatic, wrote:

---

4   George Whitefield (1714–70) was born in Gloucester of humble parents. He became a Servitor at Pembroke College, Oxford, where he came under the influence of the Wesley's in the Holy Club. A particularly clear account of the life and work of George Whitefield is found in A.A. Dallimore, *George Whitefield*, 2 vols, (Edinburgh: Banner of Truth, 1970 and 1980).

5   James Downey, *The Eighteenth Century Pulpit*, (Oxford: Clarendon, 1969), 167.

6   Heitzenrater, *Mirror and Memory: Reflections on Early Methodism,* (Nashville: Kingswood, 1989), 163.

I am very apprehensive you would stick to him as your dear brother, and so, though the Church would not excommunicate you, you would excommunicate the Church.[7]

In December 1737, upon John Wesley's leaving Georgia, Charles Wesley recruited Whitefield for work in the colony. Whitefield's ministry in Georgia was not one of his most fruitful periods; he found the work hard and slow. Returning to England in early 1739, Whitefield found it difficult to resume the work he had been doing before going to Georgia. Whilst he had been away, his sermon *On the New Birth* and his *Journals* had been published, but had not been well received. Whitefield found that he no longer owned his previous reputation and that Churches were being closed to him, as they already had been to John Wesley.

Whitefield was a determined evangelist. In February 1739 he was so moved by the desire to reach the colliers at Kingswood, Bristol, that he decided that if he could not preach inside the Church buildings, then he would preach outside them. Rupp has called this move 'the most fateful of all his [Whitefield's] adventurous initiatives.'[8] Whitefield recorded the event in his *Journal* for 17 February 1739:

> After dinner, therefore, I went upon the mount, and spake to as many people as came unto me. There were upwards of two hundred. Blessed be God that I have now broken the ice! I believe I was never more acceptable to my master than when I was standing to teach those hearers in the open fields.[9]

Whitefield was not the originator of the practice of field-preaching. Campbell has recalled that Puritan preachers practised outdoor preaching in the early seventeenth century.[10] In addition to the practice of the Welsh evangelists Howell Harris and Daniel Rowland, there was an existing tradition of such work in Kingswood and the wider Bristol area. Between 1658 and 1684 a group of Baptist preachers had worked in Bristol[11] and, in 1737, Mr Morgan, a Bristol clergyman, was known to have preached to the Kingswood miners.[12]

---

7   Baker, *Letters*, 25:681 and Telford, *Letters 1.* 3 September 1739, from the Revd Samuel Wesley, Jun.

8   E. Gordon Rupp, *Religion in England, 1688-1791*, (Oxford: OUP, 1986), 361.

9   Stuart Henry, *George Whitefield: Wayfaring Witness*, (Nashville: Abingdon, 1957), 48.

10   Ted A. Campbell, *The Religion of the Heart: A Study of European Religious Life in the Seventeenth and Eighteenth Centuries* (Columbia: University of South Carolina, 1991), 45. Campbell has suggested that it was Howell Harris who introduced Whitefield to field-preaching.

11   See W. Stephen Gunter, *The Limits of 'Love Divine'*, (Nashville: Kingswood, 1989), 140.

12   In November 1737 Whitefield had written 'Mr Morgan is going amongst the colliers again at Bristol.' A.A. Dallimore, *George Whitefield*, 1:250. It is believed that this was Richard Morgan, who had been briefly associated with John Wesley through the Oxford Holy Club. Stephen Gunter erroneously identifies the man as William Morgan who had, in

Soon after he had begun this work of field-preaching, Whitefield was called back to Georgia. He invited John Wesley to take charge of the needs of the Kingswood miners. The security and dignity that Wesley's established Church inheritance had instilled in him, made the idea of field-preaching abhorrent.

Thompson has recorded an interesting story in which it is suggested that Wesley took the question of his beginning field-preaching to the meeting of the Fetter Lane Society. It appears that some members of the Society believed that field-preaching would lead to John Wesley's death – his health being poor at the time. Thompson tells that Charles Wesley was particularly distressed; opening his Bible at random, he had come across the words of Ezekiel 24:16, 'O man, I am taking from you at one stroke the dearest thing you have, but you are not to wail or weep or give way to tears.' As was the custom of this Moravian Society, the decision was taken by the drawing of lots, the result being for Wesley to accept the invitation.[13]

Wesley, believing that the people were dying in spiritual darkness, saw the task as being so desperate that his conventional attitudes must give way. Furthermore, he believed that the law, ecclesiastical and secular, the canons and the Conventicle Act, must give way also. The Act pronounced that:

> if any person of the age of sixteen or upwards shall be present at any assembly, conventicle, or meeting, under the colour or pretence of any exercise of religion in other manner than according to the liturgy and practice of the Church of England, at which there should be five persons or more assembled together, over and beside those of the same household, if it be in a house where there is a family inhabiting, or if it be in a house, field, or place where there is not a family inhabiting, then it shall be lawful for any one or more Justices of the Peace ... or for the chief magistrate of the place ... to proceed according to the directions of the Act [to Prevent and Suppress Conventicles] and to inflict the penalties therein contained.[14]

John Wesley chose to interpret the Act according to the purpose expressed in its title, that being 'to prevent and suppress seditious conventicles.' As the Methodist gatherings were not political, seditious, or a threat to the Crown, Wesley concluded that the Act did not apply to him.[15] Having thus dispensed with the potential legal impediments, on Monday 2 April 1739 he took up the work of field-preaching. Wesley recorded the occasion in his *Journal*:

---

fact, died some years before. William Morgan was brother of Richard and had been responsible for the introduction into the Holy Club of sick and prison visiting. It was widely believed that William had died as a result of the excessive fasting and spiritual exercises practised by the Club members.

13   Edgar W. Thompson, *Wesley: Apostolic Man*, 56–57.

14   *Statutes at Large*, 18 vols, (London: 1770), 3:290–325.

15   John Wesley, *A Farther Appeal to Men of Reason and Religion, part 1* in Gerald R. Cragg, (ed.), *The Appeals to Men of Reason and Religion and Certain Related Open Letters*, in *The Works of John Wesley*, (Oxford: Clarendon, 1975), 11:183.

At four in the afternoon, I submitted to be more vile and proclaimed in the highways the
glad tidings of salvation ... The scripture on which I spoke was this, 'The Spirit of the
Lord is upon me, because he hath anointed me to preach the Gospel to the poor.'[16]

Faithfulness to the demands of his 'extraordinary' calling made it necessary for
John Wesley to step outside the Church walls and preach beyond her boundaries –
both literally and legally. Although, to some people, his actions appeared to be
little more than the dreaded enthusiasm of the period, Wesley understood himself
as having been commissioned to 'go into all the world.' The Prayer Book rubrics
and Church canons which had, so far, been Wesley's authority and guide, were put
aside in favour of the more pressing demands of the evangelical task to which he
believed himself called. Baker has written that 'An epochal change had now taken
place in his views. The work of evangelism must be furthered, Church or no
Church.'[17] Wesley wrote:

I could never reconcile myself at first to this strange way of preaching in the fields, of
which he [Whitefield] set me an example, having been all my life (till very lately) so
tenacious of every point relating to decency and order, that I should have thought the
saving of souls almost a sin, if it had not been done in a Church.[18]

Field-preaching was therefore a sudden expedient, a thing submitted to rather
than chosen, and therefore submitted to because I thought preaching even thus
better than not preaching at all.[19]

I am a creature of a day, passing through life as an arrow through the air. I am a spirit
come from God and returning to God; just hovering over the great gulf, till a few
moments hence I am no more seen – I drop into an unchangeable eternity! I want to
know one thing more, the way to heaven – how to land safe on that happy shore.[20]

It would be easy to write John Wesley off as an idiosyncratic Churchman, but
to do so would be to miss the significance of the evangelistic fervour which was
his motivating force. Wesley believed himself charged with the salvation of the
unChurched masses of the time. He felt himself uniquely called to bring the people
out of the darkness of their ignorance and challenge them with the demands of the
Gospel. The charge given him at his ordination lay heavily upon his heart. More
heavily did lie the charge he felt after his Aldersgate experience.

John Wesley's preaching within parishes to which he was not assigned led to
questions being asked about him and his methods. Albert Outler has identified that
by virtue of being ordained to Oxford University, Wesley had the right to preach

16   Curnock, *Journal*, 1:173.
17   Frank Baker, *John Wesley and the Church of England*,
(London: Epworth, 1970), 57.
18   Curnock, *Journal*, 2: 167.
19   Gerald R. Cragg, (ed.), *The Appeals,* in *Works* 11:178.
20   Albert C. Outler (ed.), *Preface* to *Sermons* in *Works* 4: 103.

throughout England. Ancient tradition gave the Chancellor of the University at Oxford the right to licence preachers to work in every diocese in England.[21] Wesley used this provision in his own defence against the bishop of Bristol in August 1739.[22]

Nevertheless, John Wesley could not rely upon the terms of the ancient provision as his sole justification. Although it answered criticism of his disregard for parish boundaries, it could not be used to justify field-preaching. In a letter to John Clayton, a former member of the Holy Club, John Wesley revealed more of his reasoning, again based upon his understanding of having received a special calling:

> I look upon all the world as my parish; thus far I mean, that in whatever part of it I am in, I judge it meet, right, and my bounden duty to declare unto all that are willing to hear the glad tidings of salvation. This is the work which I know God has called me to. And I am sure his blessing attends it.[23]

Charles Wesley was particularly sensitive to his brother's apparent lawlessness. John defended himself, by letter, on 23 June 1739.[24] Using that letter, W. Stephen Gunter has constructed a résumé of the discussion:

> The logical sequence of the statements in the letter suggests that he did not spend a great deal of time composing or rewriting the argument, but his meaning is crystal clear: 'God commands me to do good unto all men, to instruct the ignorant, reform the wicked, confirm the virtuous ... And to do this I have both ordinary call and an extraordinary [call]. My ordinary call is my ordination by the bishop: 'Take thou authority to preach the Word of God.' My extraordinary call is witnessed by the works God doth by my ministry, which prove ['evidence' in the original] that he is with me of a truth in this exercise of my office ... Man commands me not to do this in another's parish; that is, in effect, not to do it at all ... God bears witness in an extraordinary manner that my thus exercising my ordinary call is well-pleasing in his sight ... If it be just to obey man rather than God, judge ye.'[25]

John Wesley's renewed sense of vocation led to him reassessing his previous assumptions concerning Church authority and order. This was happening in June 1739 when, whilst preaching at Bath, he was confronted by Beau Nash.[26] Horrified

---

21   Outler, *Introduction, Sermons* in *Works* 1:14.

22   See below, page 19f.

23   Baker, *Letters*, 25:614 and Telford, *Letters*, 1:28, March 1739 To the Rev. John Clayton. It was previously believed that this letter had been written to James Hervey on 20 March, but the subsequent discovery of that letter disproved this theory.

24   Baker, *Letters*, 25:660 and Telford, *Letters*, 1, 23 June 1739 To the Rev. Charles Wesley.

25   W. Stephen Gunter, *The Limits of 'Love Divine'*, 142. Gunter's italics.

26   Although he was born in Swansea, Wales, Richard 'Beau' Nash is usually described as an *English* Dandy. In 1693 he held a commission in the army but made a living

at Wesley's apparent irregularity, Nash challenged him concerning his authority to preach. Wesley replied that his authority was given him by Jesus Christ at his ordination, when the bishop had laid hands on him and said, 'Take thou the authority to preach the Gospel.'[27] He looked back to his ordination as being the occasion of his having been given authority to preach. Yet, more than having been simply given authority to preach, Wesley was beginning to exhibit the marks of one who believed that the full demands of the call of God had been placed upon him.

John Wesley's words were consistent with his earlier discovery of Cyprian's teaching of the bishop being the means of conveying grace in the Church.[28] Whilst he believed himself to be preaching with the authority of Christ, Wesley understood that authority to have been given him by the bishop at his ordination. Nevertheless, Wesley was beginning to understand that the authority conveyed by the bishop might be in conflict with the authority inherent within his extraordinary calling.

When, on 18 August 1739, Wesley met with Joseph Butler, bishop of Bristol, he spoke in his own defence. The issue under discussion was Wesley's preaching in parishes to which he had not been assigned, and into which he had not been invited. He replied to the bishop:

> my business on earth is, to do what good I can. Wherever, therefore I think I can do the most good, there I must stay, so long as I think so. At present, I think I can do most good here; therefore, here I stay. As to my preaching here, a dispensation of the Gospel is committed to me, and woe is me if I preach not the Gospel, wherever I am in the habitable world. Your Lordship knows, being ordained a priest ... I am a universal priest of the Church universal; and being ordained a Fellow of a College, I was not limited to preach the word of God in any part of the Church of England.[29]

In his confrontation with the bishop, John Wesley cited the tradition that gave the Chancellor of Oxford University the right to licence preachers for work throughout England. That Wesley was willing to issue such a challenge is a further sign of his giving new priority to the authority inherent in his own calling, over and against the old authority of rubric and canon. The demand of fulfilling his 'extraordinary' calling to bring light to those who dwelt in the darkness of ignorance, was greater than the demand of faithfulness to the old expressions of authority. John Wesley had reached a position of believing that it was not a matter

---

by gambling. In 1704 he became Master of Ceremonies at Bath, where he conducted public balls with a splendour never seen before. His reforms in manners, his influence in improving the streets and buildings, and his leadership in fashion helped transform Bath into a fashionable holiday centre.

27   Curnock, *Journal*, 2:212.
28   See above, page 10.
29   Henry Moore, *The Life of the Rev John Wesley, A.M.* 2 vols, (London: John Kershaw, 1825), 1:465.

that he may preach the Gospel, but he was a man under the imperative; he must preach the Gospel.

In his justification of field-preaching and 'invading' parishes John Wesley made use of a medieval tradition to establish a distinction between settled parish ministry and the validity, in exceptional circumstances, of an irregular and informal ministry. Wesley may have come across the idea in the work of Richard Hooker[30] who wrote that God called people to acts of extraordinary ministry without requiring the Church to authorise them, 'but ... he doth ratify their calling by manifest signs and tokens himself from heaven.'[31] So it was that John Wesley pointed to the fruit of a ministry as being the test of authenticity of a call from God. He used the test of fruits in the assessment of his own action, if good fruits came only from good developments, then he could say to his brother Charles that 'My extraordinary call is witnessed by the works God doth by my ministry, which prove that he is with me ...'.[32]

It is important to remember the constant strength of Wesley's insistence that he was still a Church of England man. Although changing his interpretation of the expression of authority and practice in that Church, he did not regard himself as moving beyond her fellowship. He was seeking her spiritual enlivenment, not her demise.

Behind John Wesley's evangelistic activities lay the motivating forces of the demand for holiness and the urge for fellowship. He believed that the proper aim of every Christian life was holiness; it was the supreme offering men and women could make to God. Wesley believed the inner holiness that he desired was only to be achieved through the promotion of fellowship. Yet, he believed, fellowship was hard to find within the Church of England. He suggested that the bulk of parishioners were joined only 'as a rope of sand.'[33]

One of the results of John Wesley's preaching was the formation of religious societies. These societies were formed as 'nurture groups' for the new converts 'won' by Wesley in his field-preaching. It is important to remember that he regarded the members of the societies as being members of the Church of England. It was as societies within the Church of England that the first Methodists met together.

Wesley's societies met for fellowship, for mutual support and for Christian education. In these respects they were similar to those of earlier in the century, as

---

30   For a more detailed discussion of this, see W. Stephen Gunter, *The Limits of 'Love Divine'*, 143.

31   Richard Hooker, *On the Laws of Ecclesiastical Polity*, quoted from R.W. Church and F. Paget (eds), *The works of that Learned and Judicious Divine, Mr. Richard Hooker*, (Oxford, 1881), 169.

32   See above page 7 and W. Stephen Gunter, *The Limits of 'Love Divine'*, 142.

33   Gerald R. Cragg (ed.), *The Appeals to Men of Reason and Religion and Certain Related Open Letters, The Works of John Wesley*, (Oxford: Clarendon, 1975), 11:301, *A Farther Appeal to Men of Reason and Religion Part III.*

well as those to which the Moravians had introduced Wesley. Outler has commented that:

> Wesley's idea of the Methodist societies serving the Established Church even against the good will of her leaders was a distinctive adaptation of the pietistic patterns of the 'religious societies' (*ecclesiolae in ecclesiam*) which Anthony Horneck had brought from Germany to England in 1661 and which had served as a refuge for 'serious Christians,' discontent with apathetic and nominal Christianity.[34]

Undoubtedly, John Wesley had in mind also the meetings which took place at the Epworth Rectory during his childhood. In 1700 the Rector, Samuel Wesley, had established a Society along the lines of the SPCK. The group met in order to pray, to read the Scriptures, and to engage in spiritual discussion.

In 1711 a Society met, in the kitchen at the Epworth Rectory, under the direction of Susanna Wesley. While the Rector, John Wesley's father, was away at the meeting of Convocation, Susanna had held services for her children and servants. Her ministry was so effective that other parishioners requested permission to attend; by the end of January nearly two hundred people were present on a Sunday evening. The immediate result of her ministry was a significant increase in Church attendance and a spiritual quickening throughout Epworth.

Samuel Wesley's curate complained that Susanna was operating a clandestine conventicle and usurping the authority of her husband. When Samuel Wesley returned from London he tried to put a stop to the irregular practice, but confronted by the evidence of usefulness of the meetings he gave way to his wife. The whole affair surely made a great impression upon the young John Wesley.[35]

The Methodist Society members were subdivided into classes. The Class Meeting, which met under the direction of the Class Leader who had been appointed by Wesley from amongst the membership, was the means for closely assessing the spiritual lives of the individuals in the Society.[36] The meeting had an evangelistic function the recruitment and introduction of new members. Since the qualification for Methodist membership was not conversion but the desire for

---

34   Albert C. Outler, *John Wesley*, 307.

35   For a further discussion of the use of Religious Societies in the period see Richard P. Heitzenrater, *Mirror and Memory: Reflections on Early Methodism*, 33-45 and Richard P. Heitzenrater, *Wesley and the People Called Methodists*, (Nashville: Abingdon, 1995), 27-30. For a further discussion of Susanna Wesley's work at Epworth, see Paul W. Chilcote's two publications, *John Wesley and the Women Preachers of Early Methodism*, (Metuchen, N.J.: Scarecrow Press, 1991), 17–21 and *She offered them Christ: The Legacy of Women Preachers in Early Methodism*, (Nashville: Abingdon, 1993),18–20.

36   The development of the Methodist Class Meeting and the ministry of the Class Leader has been studied by David Lowes Watson in his two important volumes, *The Early Methodist Class Meeting: Its Origin and Significance*, (Nashville: Discipleship Resources, 1985) and *Class Leaders: Recovering a Tradition*, (Nashville: Discipleship Resources, 1991).

conversion, it followed that many were converted after they joined the Society and Class. Rather similar to the practice in the early Church though, some aspects of the life of the Methodist Societies were reserved for members only.[37]

In addition to being a means of enabling spiritual conversation, the Class Meeting was an effective method of exercising authority over the members of the Methodist Society. Those whose lives were not reflecting the fruits of conversion could be chastened and cajoled into self-improvement. Any errant member who failed to respond to the encouragement of the Class Leader could, ultimately, be effectively put out of the Society by means of withholding the renewal of the Class Ticket.

At first, John Wesley maintained personal leadership of each Methodist Society; authority for their government and direction rested entirely with him. That was the way Wesley designed it should be, for he exercised authority in a rigorously autocratic manner. However, as the number of societies increased, and John Wesley's itinerant ministry developed, it became impossible for him to retain the control he would have liked. The natural and necessary development was the appointment, by Wesley, of Assistants to provide local oversight of the societies.

---

37   The production of a current Class Ticket was, for example, the means of entrance to the Lovefeast.

Chapter 3

Wesley's Assistants
'Sons of the Gospel'

The duties of Wesley's Assistants included expounding the scriptures for the classes. One of the oft-told stories of the development of 'expounding' into 'preaching' centres upon the actions of Thomas Maxfield, the Assistant at the London Society. It was probably in 1741 that John Wesley, having to leave London, left Maxfield in charge of the Society. Maxfield took it upon himself not only to expound to the class, but to preach before the whole congregation. Filled with anger, John Wesley hastened back to reprimand Maxfield and correct the malpractice.

Wesley's initial reaction to Maxfield taking on the work of preaching reflected his constant struggle against the authority expressed through rubric and canon. His mother reminded him that he no longer accepted them as governing principles, but should test according to fruit. It took the gentle, although firm, hand of Wesley's mother to bring him back to this position. The story reveals Susanna Wesley, with characteristic equanimity, guiding her son and revealing a great depth of understanding of the ways of God:

> His mother then lived in his house, adjoining the Foundery. When he arrived, she perceived that his countenance was expressive of dissatisfaction, and inquired the cause. 'Thomas Maxfield,' said he abruptly, 'has turned Preacher, I find.' She looked attentively at him and replied, 'John, you know what my sentiments have been. You cannot suspect me of readily favouring anything of this kind. But take care what you do with respect to that young man, for he is surely called of God to preach as you are. Examine what have been the fruits of his preaching, and hear him also yourself.' He did so. His prejudice bowed before the force of truth: and he could only say, 'It is the Lord: let him do what seemeth good.'[1]

Following his mother's advice, John Wesley acted with great care. Rather than condemning Maxfield out of hand, he first went to hear him preach. Recognising that good fruit would grow from Maxfield's ministry, Wesley acknowledged the movement of the hand of God.

Thomas Maxfield was not the first lay preacher to be used by John Wesley; he was preceded in that work by John Cennick, Charles Delamotte and possibly

---

1   This is the earliest version of the story which appeared in Thomas Coke and Henry Moore, *The Life of the Rev John Wesley, A.M.* (London: Paramore, 1792), 219.

Joseph Humphreys.[2] Maxfield was, though, the first of the 'Sons of the Gospel', those converted to Christianity under the influence of John Wesley's preaching, to become an Assistant. Cennick, Delamotte and Humphries did not rise from within the Methodist revival, but merely tagged along with it. They came from within the Dissenting tradition and never became fully integrated into the Methodist connexion.

The significance of the story about Maxfield lies in his challenging Wesley's authority. Maxfield took the work upon himself without having been first authorised by John Wesley. The story is important in its demonstration of John Wesley's reaction. Initial outrage was tempered by the realisation that good fruit could come from this irregular development.

That Wesley did allow the development is a sign that no matter how irregular, or socially offensive, it appeared to be, he believed himself to be acting according to the will of God. When confronted by the conflicting demands of church authority, expressed through convention and regulation, and call of God, expressed through the urge to evangelism, Wesley believed that the church must give way to God. The ultimate test was of fruits; only good developments would lead to good fruit.

John Wesley was very clear that the Assistants were to undertake a ministry of preaching only. They were not to undertake any further development. The Assistants were expressly forbidden to engage in any sacramental ministry. They were preachers first and last. The work was not to be undertaken lightly, but only in response to the call of God. He believed it to be the extraordinary gift of God that was to be exercised with a serious sense of responsibility by an exceptional group of people.

In response to the suggestion that his use of lay preachers violated all order, John Wesley stated, categorically, that the demands of order must yield to the greater demands of the call to bring salvation to those who otherwise would die in ignorance:

> What is this order of which you speak? Will it serve instead of the knowledge and love of God? If not, how should I answer it to God, if rather than violate I know not what order, I should sacrifice thousands of souls thereto? I dare not do it. It is at the peril of my own soul.[3]

---

2   This is discussed by W. Stephen Gunter, *The Limits of 'Love Divine'*, 162 and notes. Gunter cites as evidence James Wilder, *Early Methodist Lay Preachers and their Contribution to the Eighteenth Century Revival in England,* (Ph.D. Thesis, University of Edinburgh, 1949) which, in turn, is based upon Joseph Humphrey, *An Account of Joseph Humphrey's Experience of the Work and Grace Upon his Heart,* (Bristol: Felix Harvey, 1742). Gunter also draws the reader's attention to Luke Tyerman, *Leaves of an Overlooked Chapter in Methodist History; or Wesley's (Reputed) 'First Lay-Preacher'*, in Wesleyan Methodist Magazine, 108 (1884): 90–9, 193–201, 277–85.

3   John Wesley, *A Farther Appeal* in *Works,* 11:300.

Information about John Wesley's appointment of his preachers, which was always conducted in private, is available to us through the autobiographies which he required those associated with him to write. Thomas Jackson and John Telford have collected many of these autobiographies in their multi–volumed works.[4] When appointing the preachers, Wesley did not use a liturgical text; it is then difficult to know exactly what he did. However, through the work of Jackson and Telford, we have available to us a number of accounts which enable us to point to the variety of Wesley's practice. A few of these accounts relate the occasions of Methodists being interviewed and appointed to work by John Wesley.

One of the clearest accounts of being interviewed and appointed is given by Joseph Cownley who, in 1746, met with John Wesley at Bristol. At the climax of that interview Cownley knelt down, and Wesley, putting the New Testament into his hand, said, 'Take thou authority to preach the Gospel.' Wesley then gave Cownley his benediction. Thus authorised, Cownley went on his way.[5]

Adam Clarke was, similarly, interviewed by John Wesley on 6 September 1782. Clarke records that Wesley took him kindly by the hand, and said, 'Well, brother Clarke, do you wish to devote yourself entirely to the work of God?' After Clarke had affirmed that he wished to do and be whatever pleased God, Wesley replied, 'We want a preacher for Bradford; hold yourself in readiness to go thither.' Etheridge, Clarke's biographer, continued with the account:

> He then turned to me, laid his hands upon my head, and spent a few moments in praying to God to bless and preserve me, and to give me success in the work to which I was called. I departed, having now received, in addition to my appointment from God to preach this Gospel, the only authority I could from a man, in that I can exercise the ministry of the Divine Word.[6]

Often the ministry of the Methodists developed naturally, with candidates progressing from the lower levels of leadership in the societies. An anonymous critic, recognising this practice, has written:

> No sooner does a person commence Methodist; than he may hope to rise through all the different gradations of the Society, and may even aspire to become in time a travelling preacher.[7]

---

4   Thomas Jackson, *Lives of the Early Methodist Preachers*, 6 vols, (London: John Mason, 1837–38) and John Telford, *Wesley Veterans: Lives of the Early Methodist Preachers,* 7 vols, (London: Epworth, 1912–14).

5   Telford, *Wesley Veterans*, 4:128.

6   J.W. Etheridge, *The Life of the Rev. Adam Clark*, (London: John Mason, 1858), 55.

7   Anon, *A Review of the Policy, Doctrines and Morals of the Methodists*, (London: Johnson, 1791), 8.

Sometimes John Wesley dispensed with the formalities of an interview, preferring instead to simply appoint people from other positions to the work of preaching. Because the people were already working with him, and thus known to him, Wesley felt able to make such appointments without the interview. This was the experience of John Pritchard, who recounted in his autobiography that he had previously been appointed as a class leader, but:

> after being at Kingswood some time, I received a letter from you, desiring me to go immediately into the Wiltshire Circuit. This threw me into a fever, and brought on me much trouble of mind; seeing I was weak in grace and gifts, and young in years, as well as of shy disposition. However, I ventured.[8]

Matthias Joyce was similarly appointed by letter. In 1773, after hearing Wesley preach in Dublin, Joyce had been impressed into becoming more constant in attending the Society and in practising private devotion. In 1782 Joyce felt a call to preach, but at first there had been some objection to him. Later the same year, following the intervention of a number of people, John Wesley appointed him on trial. Although it is not stated, it can be assumed that this took place after John Wesley had met with Joyce. It is unlikely that Wesley would have appointed somebody unknown to him, especially after there had been questions raised against them. Joyce recounted his story:

> it was impressed on my mind that I ought to give myself up to the blessed work of calling sinners to repentance... At first some objection was made to me, on account of my family. But about Christmas 1782, I received a letter from Mr. Wesley, the substance of which was as follows:

> Dear Brother,
> Not only Mr Smith, but several others, gave satisfactory account of you at the Conference. Mr Watkinson writes me word that as Robert Blake has left him, he is in great want of help. I have no objection, if your wife is willing, for you to go on trial to Limerick.[9]

The pattern, which can be seen, was that the people would become aware of a sense of call, but often received it with reluctance or resistance. This sense of call would grow in strength until those who felt it realised that they must do something about it. Often their first act would be to consult with fellow members of the Society. John Wesley was willing to help those who felt a call to preach to work through the process of discovering whether that call was fitting. Thomas Walsh benefited from such help; uncertain of his call he sought the advice of Wesley. The reply came:

8   Telford, *Wesley Veterans*, 4:208.
9   Telford, *Wesley Veterans*, 7:238.

It is hard to judge what God has called you to, till trial is made. Therefore, when you have an opportunity, you may go to Shronell, and spend two or three days with the people there. Speak to them in Irish.[10]

Wesley believed that the best test of a call to preach was to try preaching. He allowed such as felt called to offer to be one of his Assistants to test that call by trying their hand at the work. The principle of authenticity of call being measured by its fruits was a useful guide to John Wesley in such matters. Cragg has suggested that John Wesley was 'appealing to the example of the Reformed churches, but he was unquestionably aware of the use of *facultas* in churches of the Catholic tradition.'[11]

The account told by Thomas Taylor further illustrated the experience of being interviewed by John Wesley, and of being appointed as one of his Assistants:

> The Summer being arrived, and Mr. Wesley coming into the country, I met him at Birstall (17 July 1761). He received me with that affability and condescension for which he is remarkable ... As the Conference was drawing near he advised me to attend it at London. I intimated a desire of spending a year in that place, that I might be fully informed both in the doctrines and discipline of the Methodists. Accordingly, I disposed of some small effects which I had, and set out on foot. When I came thither I expected to undergo a close examination, with regard to my principles, experience and abilities; and therefore, as I did not in everything agree with Mr. Wesley, it was a doubt with me whether I should not be rejected. But, to my surprise, I was not asked one question relative to any of these things; but was appointed for Wales, and was the only travelling preacher of our connexion in those parts. This I have sometimes thought was not prudently done, as I was but just come into the connexion.[12]

Such is the scant evidence as survives on this matter. It all points towards a somewhat haphazard and ad hoc arrangement. That these events were not ordinations does not seem to have always occurred to some of those who have commented upon them. In particular, Adam Clarke's biographer, J.W. Etheridge, referred to the event as Clarke's ordination.[13]

It is clear, then, that John Wesley had no intention for his preachers to expand their work beyond that of proclaiming the Gospel. His intention, when separating them, was that they were being set apart for the work of preaching. It is important to recognise this intention in attempting to understand Wesley's mind on the matter. Richard Watson, Wesley's nineteenth-century biographer, was wrong in his assertion that John Wesley intended ordination.[14]

Putting the intention of John Wesley alongside his authority, one concludes that no matter how he expressed himself at the time, or how those associated with him

---

10   Telford, *Wesley Veterans*, 5:34.
11   Gerald R. Cragg, *The Appeals* in *Works*, 11:298.
12   Telford, *Wesley Veterans*, 7:25.
13   J.W. Etheridge, *The Life of the Rev. Adam Clark*, (London: John Mason,1858), 55.
14   Richard Watson, *The Life of John Wesley*, (London: John Mason, 1831), 204.

understood the charge being placed upon them, John Wesley did not ordain them, because he said that he did not.

Although John Wesley had no particular preference for the manner in which he initiated his new workers, a pattern can be traced. He required that the prospective preachers should, unless personally known to him, present themselves for interview before him. Always he prayed for them, but sometimes he did so having placed his hand in benediction upon their head. Sometimes he gave the Bible and uttered the formula, 'Take thou authority to preach the Gospel.'

The appointment and employment of John Wesley's Assistants and preachers echoed that of the diaconal ministers as Assistants to the local bishop in the early church. Primitive Christianity understood the deacon, rather than the priest/presbyter, as the alternative 'minister' in the absence of the bishop. The tradition of deacons being ordained by the bishop, at whose direction and in relationship with whom they were to work, arose from this understanding. It can then be claimed that there were historic precedents in John Wesley's appointment of his Assistants. However, unlike that diaconal ordination, John Wesley did not intend the appointment to be the action of the whole Church. He appointed them as his own subordinates, he assigned them to their position, they were to work only in relationship with him, for he was their scriptural *episcopos*.

It is clear that in appointing his work force John Wesley gave them authority to perform the work of preaching the Gospel amongst the Methodist Societies already in existence. Usually, upon appointment, they were sent immediately to work in a specified Society. He gave them authority for no other work, neither of evangelisation beyond the Society, nor for the administration of the sacraments. They were charged solely with the task of acting as 'under-shepherds' of Wesley's flock. Nor was there any sense of indelibility attached to the appointment of the preachers. They were appointed out of expediency and they could be removed from the work, without redress, according to the whims of Wesley's autocratic exercise of authority.

John Wesley regarded his preachers as being 'extraordinary' messengers called to 'provoke to jealousy the ordinary messengers.'[15] His purpose was the enlivenment of the Church of England. He regarded the use of his lay preachers as a temporary expedient towards that end. They were 'interim' ministers who were intended to provoke the 'ordinary' ministers, the priests of the established church, into action. Presumably, John Wesley anticipated that once the established church began to respond to his spiritual challenge then his workers would become redundant. Such an intention necessitated a form of appointment and supervision which would enable a prompt and tidy removal of his 'extraordinary' workforce.

The appointment of the first preachers was an event which took place in the formal atmosphere of the private interview with John Wesley. It was not a public liturgical event. The event represented John Wesley appointing those who were to

---

15   John Wesley's Sermon on *Prophets and Priests*, Albert C. Outler (ed.), *Sermons IV (115–51)* in *The Works of John Wesley*, (Nashville: Abingdon, 1987), 4:82.

be his personal Assistants, it was not the public act of a church engaging in separating, authorising or ordaining her ministers. John Wesley, the autocrat, undertook sole responsibility for the selection and appointment of those who would work, at his direction, as his Assistants. Called of God they certainly were, but that they were solely accountable to John Wesley was equally certain.

All churches raise up their leaders from within the ranks of their membership. John Wesley's practice followed this pattern; those appointed to be his preachers were all members of the Methodist societies. Methodism, though, created a variety of leadership opportunities for those who would not normally have been called to such work. As Chilcote has suggested, Methodism was particularly active in providing 'a sense of empowerment for those who stood impotently on the periphery of English Society.'[16]

The Methodist lay leaders were largely drawn from the masses of working class and common people for whom Methodism held particular appeal. John Wesley's preachers and Assistants were not the educated élite who would, for example, be found amongst the leadership of the established church. They were, more usually, uncomplicated artisans who had been enlivened and empowered by a sense of the presence of the living God acting in their lives. They were required to hold no qualification save that of a sense of call from God evidenced by a growth in wisdom and grace.

Sometimes the Methodist people were subjected to ridicule and teasing. Their often limited educational background made it difficult for them to exercise the gift of discernment. There is a story told of an unsophisticated Methodist who was duped into believing he had heard the call of God to travel to America:

> A very remarkable instance of this enthusiastic turn, is told of a Methodist, who lived with his family, in pretty easy circumstances, in a populous town in the North of England. Nothing would please but being a preacher, and, like many others of his profession, he believed he had an immediate call from the spirit. One night, an arch wag that lived by, who knew the crazy fool's foible, and had a mind to give him an American voyage, concealed himself in a barn, or stable, where he knew he used to come and say his prayers. After he came, and entered on his favourite topic asking the Lord to give him a manifest token that he had called him to preach the gospel; the fellow, who lay concealed, judging this a fit time to break silence, desired him, with a counterfeit voice, to arise, and go and Preach the gospel in America, for the Lord had much work for him there. The poor frantic enthusiast hearing this with pleasure and surprise, ran and told his family, and, in spite of their tears and solicitations, set out the next day, charmed with his imagined heavenly message, while the other laughed in his sleeve, and told the trick among his merry companions, after the poor fool was gone.[17]

---

16   Paul Wesley Chilcote, *John Wesley and the Women Preachers of Early Methodism*, 67.

17   Calvinisticus, *Calvinism Defended and Arminianism Refuted*, (Leeds: Binns, 1780), 4.

The canons of the Church of England had, in 1604, made provision for the continuance of the medieval practice of only licensing those preachers who were believed to be sufficiently qualified academically. In the seventeenth century not all priests had been sufficiently well educated to be licensed to preach.[18] Remembering this condition, many eighteenth–century Church leaders pronounced that, even if they applied for regular licensing, the majority of Methodist Assistants ought not to be allowed to preach.

The lack of formal education on the part of many of the preachers led to their being caricatured as 'ignorant and illiterate mechanics.' In 1745, there was criticism from Dr Thomas Rutherford, Regius Professor of Divinity at Cambridge, that the Methodist preachers were ignorant. In his reply, John Wesley stated that they were not all ignorant, and that he believed many of them could successfully undergo examination for orders.

> Indeed in the one thing which they profess to know they are not ignorant men. I trust there is not one of them who is not able to go through such an examination in substantial, practical, experimental divinity, as few of our candidates or holy orders, even in the university (I speak it in sorrow and shame, and in tender love) are able to do … But they are laymen.[19]

The ridicule to which the early Methodists were subjected was partly due to the fact that many were indeed ignorant in the things normally associated with a University education – then the usual qualification for ordination into the Church of England. Many of the objections against the Methodist movement were founded upon this use of unordained Assistants; the following letter, written by John Wesley to an unspecified clergyman, outlined the situation:

> Will you object, 'But he is no minister, nor has any authority to save souls'? I must beg leave to dissent from you in this. I think he is a true, evangelical minister, διάκουσο, servant of Christ and His church, who ουτο διάκουέι, so ministers, as to save souls from death, to reclaim sinners from their sins; and that every Christian, if he is able to do it, has authority to save a dying soul. But, if you only mean he has no authority to take tithes, I grant it. He takes none; as he has freely received, so he freely gives … I am afraid that reasonable men will be much inclined to think he that saves souls is no minister of Christ … 'Oh, but he is ordained, and therefore has authority.' Authority to do what? 'To save all the souls that will put themselves under his care.' True; but (to waive the case of them that will not; and would you desire that even those should perish?) he does not, in fact, save them that are under his care.[20]

---

18   G.R. Evans and J. Robert Wright, *The Anglican Tradition: A Handbook of Sources*, 198–9.

19   Gerald R. Cragg, *The Appeals* in *Works*, 11:296.

20   Telford, *Letters*, 2:148–49. 'Letter to a clergyman' 4 May 1748.

In a letter dated 18 September 1756, to James Clark, John Wesley explained his conviction that a call from God, rather than licence of a bishop, made a preacher. The discussion drew attention to the Twenty–Third article which states that only those called and permitted by the church authorities are allowed to exercise a ministry of either preaching or administering the sacraments:

> I believe several who are not episcopally ordained are nevertheless called of God to preach the Gospel. Yet I have no exception to the Twenty-third article, though I judge there are exempt cases. That the seven deacons were outwardly ordained to that low office cannot be denied; but when Paul and Barnabas were separated for the work to which they were called, this was not ordaining them. St. Paul was ordained long before, and that not of man nor by men. It was inducting him into the province for which our Lord had appointed him from the beginning. For this end the prophets and teachers fasted and prayed and laid their hands upon them – a rite which was used, not in ordination only, but in blessing and many other occasions.[21]

In the same letter Wesley exclaimed that a lay preacher was surely to be preferred to a drunken, cursing, swearing preacher.[22] Wesley's main consideration was the preaching of the Gospel for the salvation of souls. The necessity of proclaiming the Gospel was John Wesley's motivation for using unordained preachers, especially 'where thousands are rushing to destruction, and those who are ordained and appointed to watch over them neither care for nor know how to help them.'[23]

John Green, bishop of Lincoln wrote, in 1760, that the Methodists had set themselves free from the old understanding that only the educated ought to preach, but, he suggested it was highly presumptuous for any to preach at all, unless they had been ordained.[24] He recognised that the Methodists supposed that anyone who had been given the gift of utterance was qualified to preach the Gospel, even the ignorant:

---

21   Telford, *Letters*, 3:200. To James Clark, 18 September 1756.

22   Telford, *Letters*, 3:203. To James Clark, 18 September 1756. A theme repeated in John Wesley's letter to Dr Rutherford, Telford, *Letters*, 5:361, 28 March 1768.

23   Telford, *Letters*, 4:150. To the Earl of Dartmouth, 10 April 1761.

24   John Green, *The Principles and Practices of the Methodists Considered in some Letters to the readers of that Sect. The first addresses to the Reverend Mr. B___e. Wherein are some remarks on his Two Letters to a Clergyman in Nottinghamshire, lately published. Under the pseudonym Academicus.* (London: W. Bristow, 1760). 8–11. Again referring to the Medieval tradition continued in the Canons of 1604 which provided that only suitably qualified priests were licensed to preach.

How rapid too and vehement must be the efforts of this passion, when all a man's powers are called forth, all his zeal and vigour excited, all his designs and resolutions animated by the fullest conviction, that he is acting under the express direction of Heaven, and let to execute, what he undertakes, by the immediate finger of God? [25]

Further defending the use of lay preachers, in relation to the Twenty-Third Article, Wesley's letter to the Earl of Dartmouth, 10 April 1761 stated:

They subscribed it in the simplicity of their hearts, when they firmly believed none but Episcopal ordination valid. But bishop Stillingfleet has since fully convinced them this was an entire mistake.[26]

Writing in 1768, Wesley again answered Rutherford:

Most of the travelling preachers in connexion with me are not ignorant men. As I observed before, they know all which they profess to know. The languages they do not profess to know; yet some of them understand them well. Philosophy they do not profess to know; yet some of them tolerably understand this also. They understand both one and the other better than a great part of my pupils at the university did.[27]

George L. Fleury, archdeacon of Waterford, was critical of the Methodist movement:

Another fundamental error of the Methodists is the asserting that laymen may preach, yea the most ignorant and illiterate of them, provided they have an inward call of the spirit.[28]

John Wesley's reply outlined the more accurate assertion that:

They do not allow the 'most ignorant' men to preach whatever 'inward call' they pretend to. Among them none are allowed to be stated preachers but such as: (1) Are truly alive to God, such as experience the 'faith that worketh by love' such as love God and all mankind; (2) Such as have a competent knowledge of the word of God and of the work of God in the souls of men; (3) Such as have given proof that they are called of God by converting sinners from the error of their ways. And to show whether they have these qualifications or no, they are a year, sometimes more, upon trial. Now I pray, what is the common examination either for deacon's or priest's orders to this.[29]

---

25   John Green, *The Principles and Practices of the Methodists Considered in some Letters to the readers of that Sect. The first addresses to the Reverend Mr. B___e. Wherein are some remarks on his Two Letters to a Clergyman in Nottinghamshire, lately published. Under the pseudonym Academicus.* (London: W. Bristow, 1760). 8–11.

26   Telford, *Letters*, 4:150. To the Earl of Dartmouth, 10 April 1761.

27   Telford, *Letters*, 5:362. To Dr. Rutherford, 28 March 1768.

28   Curnock, *Journal*, 5:244, 18 May 1771.

29   Telford, *Letters*, 5:249. 'To George L. Fleury', 18 May 1771.

Charles Wesley wrote a satirical poem concerning his brother John's attitude towards his lay leaders and preachers. From the words, one can assume that Charles was less than certain about the security of his brother's ground.

All my Geese are Swans.[30]

> The Methodists must allow
> Their Preachers taken from the Plough;
> In Schools they pick'd up little knowledge,
> Nothing beholden to the College;
> To Science they had no Pretence,
> To dress, or Taste, or Elegance;
> To labour, not to Learned bred,
> Yet most of them could write & read;
> And some, by Mother's care, knew how
> To doff their hats, & make a Bow.
>
> Small their Acquaintance with their Betters,
> With Men of Fashion, or of Letters;
> They aim'd at no Distinction here,
> Of Place, or Rank, or Character.
>
> But lo! thro' a fond Father's Aid
> They all at once become well-bred;
> And instantaneously polite;
> Spring up like Mushrooms in the night;
> Equals to Men of high degre, [Sic]
> The very Pink of Courtesy;
> Worthy superlative Esteem,
> For why? – they all belong to HIM
> Whose ev'ry Goose is a black Swan,
> Whose ev'ry Jack's a Gentleman.

One of Wesley's contemporaries, Haddon Smith, observed that the Methodist belief that the Holy Spirit provided them with all necessary wisdom led them to assert that 'Human Learning is ... to be cried down as unnecessary ... to the encouragement of every illiterate Carman or Porter to set himself up as a preacher.'[31] At a time when the Church of England clergy were following the demands of rationalism, this supposed attitude of the Methodists did not go down well.

---

30   S.T. Kimbrough, Jr and Oliver A. Beckerlegge (eds) *The Unpublished Poetry of Charles Wesley*, Vol. 3, *Hymns and Poems for Church and World.* (Nashville: Kingswood, 1992), 82.
31   Haddon Smith, *Methodistical Deceit: A sermon preached in the Parish Church of St. Matthew, Bethnal Green, Middlesex,* (London: H. Turpin, 1770), 4–5.

A.M. Lyles reported that one of the critics of the Methodists was irritated when his parish was invaded by a Methodist preacher who:

> came to an Anglican parish in the spirit, and with the language of a missionary going to the most ignorant heathens; and he asked the clergyman to lend him his pulpit, in order that he might instruct his parishioners for the first time on the true Gospel of Christ.[32]

The anonymous poet who became known as 'Author of *The Saints*' was shameless in his caricature of the early Methodist preachers:

> As ably to the 'Chosen Few' laid down
> In 'leathen Apron' as in 'Band and Gown.'
> No saving Truths to them so plain appear
> As when a 'Cobbler's' Comment makes 'em clear.[33]

John Wesley's understanding of the purpose and work of the Christian ministry remained clearly defined. He believed that a minister of the Gospel was commissioned to work for the salvation of the souls of all people, and in that work must spend and be spent. The minister was required to have a good grounding in secular as well as spiritual knowledge. Furthermore, gifts from God were required; single intention, affection for those to whom they minister, the practice of a good life. The minister's life was to be lived for the 'bringing of many to glory.' They were envoys and ambassadors.[34]

John Wesley, recalling the words of the ordaining bishop, 'Receive the Holy Ghost,' reminded his fellow clergy that they ministered the word and sacraments before God. He added that God had given the Holy Spirit to those who have received their ministry, so that through their hands the Holy Spirit was given to others. Writing to his brother Charles on 26 April 1772, John Wesley stated:

> Your business, as well as mine, is to save souls. When we took priests' orders, we undertook to make it our one business. I think every day lost which is not (mainly at least) employed in this thing; *sum totus in illo*.[35]

John Wesley regarded the real test of his ministry to be the measurement of its practical results. That a minister do the work of an evangelist and make full proof of that ministry was determined by the number of people turned to righteousness. He believed himself to be doing the work of any true minister of the Gospel. As a clergyman of the established church he maintained that he remained faithful to the

---

32   A.M. Lyles, *Methodism Mocked: The Satiric Reaction to Methodism in the Eighteenth Century*, (London: Epworth, 1960), 28.

33   Author of the Saints, *The Fanatic Saints; or Bedlamites Inspired. A Satire*, (London: J. Bew, 1778), 6.

34   Jackson, *Works*, 10:480, Address to the Clergy.

35   Telford, *Letters*, 5:316. To Charles Wesley, 26 April 1772. ('*Sum totus in illo*' is from Horace's *Satires*, 1.ix.2 ('*Totus in illis*'): 'I am entirely occupied with it.')

church of his ordination. But Wesley believed that ecclesiastical status was a minor matter by comparison with the urgency of this task. He wrote to Alexander Mather:

> Give me one hundred preachers who fear nothing but sin and desire nothing but God, and I care not a straw whether they be clergymen or laymen, such alone will shake the gates of hell and set up the kingdom of heaven upon earth.[36]

John Wesley spared no effort in the defence of his use of lay preachers. Some pride was noticeable as Wesley quoted Archbishop Potter, in a letter to the *Dublin Chronicle,* saying that the Methodist preachers 'are irregular; but they have done good, and I pray God to bless them.'[37]

The clergy of the Church of England continued to keep John Wesley and his associates from entering their buildings, forcing them to preach in the open air. The criticisms of Methodism multiplied. Irregularities such as field-preaching, lay preachers, societies dividing parishes, as well as imagined doctrinal deviations, were brought under the scrutiny of the establishment at large. Lay preaching in particular seemed, to many critics, to be so contrary to Church of England order as to constitute schism and separation. Gunter has written:

> The total lack of appreciation for learning on the part of many produced a class of preachers who were often caricatured as ignorant, illiterate mechanics. These practitioners of religious zeal were known to move freely from village to village and county to county preaching at the drop of a hat. It became a very sensitive issue that Wesley and his preachers, following Whitefield's example, even resorted to preaching in the open air, a clear violation of the law in the minds of most Anglicans. Thomas Church lamented, 'Now, supposing that there is no express law against this, yet the … act of toleration strongly prohibits it. It orders all places of worship to be licensed. And you cannot pretend, that the fields you have assembled in are so … fields cannot be licensed for these purposes …[38]

Most of the leaders of the Church of England believed that the value of the Methodist preachers was negligible and that the movement was the embodiment of lawlessness. It is not surprising that the early Methodist Conferences, from 1744 to 1747, spent much time in the discussion of discipline, not only for its own sake but also in terms of relationships with the Church of England. The Conference of 1747 confirmed a threefold test of those who felt themselves called to preach:

---

36   Telford, *Letters*, 5:272. To Alexander Mather. 6 August 1777.
37   Telford, *Letters*, 8:141. To the printer of *The Dublin Chronicle*, 2 June 1789.
38   W. Stephen Gunter, *The Limits of 'Love Divine'*, 32. Quoting from Thomas Church, *A Serious and Expostulatory Letter to the Rev. Mr. George Whitefield*, (London: M. Cooper, 1744), 32.

1) Do they know in whom they have believed? Have they the love of God in their hearts? Do they desire and seek nothing but God? And are they holy in all manner of conversation?

2) Have they gifts (As well as Grace) for the work? Have they (in some tolerable degree) a clear sound understanding? Have they a right judgement in the things of God? Have they a just conception of the salvation by faith? And has God given them any degree of utterance? Do they speak justly, readily, clearly?

3) Have they success? Do they not only so speak as generally either to convince or affect the hearts? But have any received remission of sins by their preaching? A clear and lasting sense of the love of God? As long as these three marks undeniably concur in any, we allow him to be called of God to preach. These we receive as sufficient reasonable evidence that he is moved thereto by the Holy Ghost.[39]

It can be seen that John Wesley was putting his former views of the source and expression of authority alongside the demands of his 'extraordinary' calling. He realised that he had to keep a strict account of the work of those associated with him, lest he descend to the unappealing depths of Dissent. The purpose of his work was the enlivenment of the Church of England, not the establishment of a new Church. It was necessary that John Wesley take great care in his use of Assistants; he must retain to himself the control of the movement.

---

39   *Minutes*, (London: Charles H. Kelly, 1896), 35.

Chapter 4

Wesley's Expression of Authority
'I am a Scriptural Episcopos'

The first Methodist Conference, which met in 1744, considered the question of how far it was the duty of Methodists to obey the Church of England bishops. The Conference, that is to say John Wesley, concluded that they should obey them, 'in all things indifferent. And on this ground of obeying them, we should observe the canons, so far as we can with a safe conscience.'[1]

The expression of ministry, understanding of authority, and the practice of order, within early Methodism, was closely related to John Wesley's understanding of the nature of the church. He considered the Methodist people to be that 'congregation of faithful men,' amongst whom the Nineteenth Article tells that 'the pure word of God is preached and the sacraments duly administered.' Rather than being separate from the Church of England, the early Methodists were being encouraged to regard themselves as the purest expression of that Church.

Henry Rack has suggested that the Methodists' understanding of the Nineteenth Article enabled them to ignore the whole question of establishment, canon law and all that went with the Church of England. They considered themselves free to assert that membership and zeal for the Church was a matter of upholding Christian truth and life; they were to obey the bishops only in 'things indifferent' and they did not separate so long as they preached the Church's doctrines and attended its worship.[2] Bringing to mind John Wesley's comment that 'the clergy who do not preach the Gospel are really the worse dissenters from the church,'[3] Dr. Rack added the observation that the situation, in some ways, recalled:

> an almost Anabaptist vision of the church, in others it echoes back to the Anglican Puritans of an earlier period and forward to the rebellious Tractarians of a later. At the time it clearly reflects Wesley's polemic against contemporary clergy, whom he felt were betraying the Church of England's true Gospel far more than he was and therefore were practically separating from it, as he was not.[4]

In August 1745, the second Methodist Conference continued the discussion of, and also raised further questions concerning, church government. In answering the

---

1   *Minutes*, 13.
2   Henry Rack, *Reasonable Enthusiast*, 293.
3   Curnock, *Journal*, 2:335.
4   Henry Rack, *Reasonable Enthusiast*, 293.

question, 'Is Episcopal, Presbyterian, or Independent church-government most agreeable to reason?' John Wesley stated:

> The plain origin of Church-government seems to be this. Christ sends forth a preacher of the Gospel. Some who hear him repent and believe the Gospel. They then desire him to watch over them, to build them up in faith, and to guide their souls in the paths of righteousness. Here then is an independent congregation, subject to no pastor but their own, neither liable to be controlled in things spiritual by any other man or body of men whatsoever.

> But soon after some from other parts, who are occasionally present while he speaks in the name of him that sent him, beseech him to come over and help them also. Knowing it to be the will of God he consents (complies), yet not till he has conferred with the wisest and holiest of his congregation, and with their advice appointed one who had gifts and grace to watch over the flock till his return.

> If it please God to raise another flock in that place, before he leaves them he does the same thing, appointing one whom God has fitted for the work to watch over these souls. In like manner, in every place where it pleases God to gather a little flock by his word, he appoints one in his absence to take the oversight of the rest, and to assist them of the ability which God giveth. These are Deacons, or servants of the church, and look on their first pastor as their common father. And all these congregations regard him in the light, and esteem him still as the shepherd of their souls.

> These congregations are not strictly independent. They depend on one pastor, though not on each other.

> As these congregations increase, and as the Deacons grow in years and grace, they need other subordinate Deacons or helpers; in respect of whom they may be called Presbyters, or Elders, as their father in the Lord may be called the bishop or overseer of them all.[5]

Thus in answering the question, Wesley sketched an historical account of how church order developed by natural processes when a preacher collected a congregation and then evolved in succession through independent, presbyterian and episcopal polities. The description fitted the manner in which Methodism arose, with authority vested in Wesley as the one who initiated the process. At the same time the scheme offered a naturalistic explanation of the rise of the Christian ministry as such, which by implication disposed of any of the main forms of church order as being exclusively of divine ordinance. It was a description that portrayed the manner in which Methodism came into being, with authority vested in John Wesley as the initiator of the process. The picture presented was of a great

---

5   Although there are no printed minutes of the Wesleyan Conferences before 1749, records of the first five Conferences have survived in manuscript form. This account from 1745 is published in Rupert Davies, A. Raymond George, Gordon Rupp, (eds) *A History of the Methodist Church in Great Britain*, 4 vols, (London: Epworth, 1965–88), 4:77.

religious movement with John Wesley, the scriptural *episcopos*, at its head, leading, directing and governing.

When reviewing ancient Christianity, John Wesley believed the influence of Constantine to have been less worthy than normally accepted. He believed that the emperor's donation of wealth to the church, and his giving honour to the Christians, led to the church's moral decline. He believed that the church became mixed with paganism, and thus Christians became 'lovers of the world, lovers of themselves, lovers of pleasure more than lovers of God.' The clergy began to seek wealth and power, and ministerial orders, formerly divided according to a number of functions, were consolidated under the office of bishop.[6]

Following ancient Christianity, John Wesley distinguished the 'extraordinary' ministry of those who preached from the 'ordinary' ministry of those who maintained order and administered the sacraments.[7] So it was that on 27 December 1745, John Wesley wrote to Westley Hall, his brother-in-law:

> We believe it would not be right for us to administer either Baptism or the Lord's Supper unless we had a commission so to do from those bishops whom we apprehend to be in a succession from the apostles. And yet we allow, these bishops are successors of those who were dependent on the Bishop of Rome.[8]

John Wesley thus affirmed his belief in the apostolic succession of bishops in such a manner as to question the validity of sacraments administered by clergy not ordained by bishops in that succession. At this time, then, his view of episcopacy, and of the power of ordination, coincided with that of the conservative 'Caroline' theologians of the seventeenth century.[9] Soon afterwards, however, Wesley's conceptions of the ancient episcopate began to change.

An entry in John Wesley's *Journal* for 20 January 1746 marked the point at which he entered a new phase of thought in his theology of ministry. The entry recorded Wesley as having read, and been impressed by, Lord Peter King's *An Enquiry into the Constitution, Discipline, Unity and Worship of The Primitive*

---

6   For a full discussion, see Ted A. Campbell, *John Wesley and Christian Antiquity*, 47–51.

7   His edition of Mosheim's *Concise Ecclesiastical History* included a passage identifying the 'Extraordinary teachers' as being the twelve apostles and the seventy disciples who were needed to establish the church, as being distinct from the 'ordinary ministers' who enforced and maintained the doctrine. Mosheim, *Concise Ecclesiastical History*, ED. Wesley, I:II:II:1–3 (1781 edn, 1:55–56) But compare with Wesley's edition of Fleury, *Manners of the Ancient Christians*, 1:10 (1798 edn, p.6) where the apostles and the seventy are simply distinguished from the laity as those 'set apart for ministry in public'.

8   Baker, *Letters*, 2:173. 27 December 1745 'To Westley Hall'.

9   The seventeenth century, said by some to be 'The Golden Age' of Anglicanism, produced a collection of theologians who are known as the 'Caroline' Divines. This group included Lancelot Andrewes, William Laud, Thomas Ken, Anthony Sparrow and Herbert Thorndike.

Church. Wesley read King's work whilst travelling to Bristol; he recounted the experience:

> I set out for Bristol and read over Lord King's 'Account of the Primitive Church'. In spite of the vehement prejudice of my education, I was ready to believe that this was a fair and impartial draught; but, if so, it would follow that bishops and presbyters are (essentially) of one order, and that originally every Christian congregation was a church independent of all others.[10]

Peter King[11] suggested that there were two constituent parts of the church, clergy and laity. His thesis dealt with the acts of clergy as differing from those of the laity and, then, the joint acts of both. King recalled that in antiquity the bishop was the normal minister in every congregation. Bishops were to be found not only in cities but also in the country villages, provided there were enough believers to constitute a congregation. King defined a presbyter as a person in holy orders, having thereby an inherent right to perform the whole office of a bishop; but being possessed of no place or parish, not actually discharging it, without the permission and consent of the bishop of a place or parish.

> Lest this definition should seem obscure I shall illustrate it by this following instance: as a curate hath the same mission and power with a minister, whose place he supplies; yet being not the minister of that place, he cannot perform there any acts of his ministerial function, without leave from the minister thereof; so a presbyter had the same order and power with a bishop, whom he assisted in his cure … he could not perform any parts of his pastoral office without the permission of a bishop.[12]

Whilst King felt it to be necessarily proved that a presbyter could perform any office normally carried out by a bishop, he admitted that it could not be particularly proved that a presbyter did actually discharge every one of them. They could only do so with the bishop's permission.

King further defined his understanding of ordination in the primitive church:

> That ordination I shall speak of, is this, the grant of a peculiar commission and power, which remains indelible in the person to whom it is committed, and can never be obliterated or erased out, except the person himself cause it by his heresy, apostasy, or most gross and scandalous impiety. Now this sort of ordination was conferred only upon deacons and presbyters, or on deacons and bishops, presbyters and bishops being here to be considered as all one, as ministers of the universal church.[13]

John Wesley took two points from King. First, that bishops and presbyters were essentially of one 'order' (*ordo*), although bishops were a higher 'degree' (*gradus*) of presbyters. Second, confirming his position as outlined in the 1745 Conference, that every congregation was originally independent of all others. The likelihood of

---

10 Curnock, *Journal*, 3:232.
11 Born in 1669, Peter King was a nephew of John Locke.
12 Peter King, *An Enquiry into the Constitution, Discipline, Unity and Worship of The Primitive Church,* (London, 1691), 53.
13 Peter King, *An Enquiry*, 83.

Wesley, whilst reading one book, experiencing anything which would compel an immediate remodelling of his well established theology of authority and order, is remote. The process was altogether more protracted. King's work was undoubtedly influential and significant, but only as a milestone, or signpost, is significant on a long journey. Curnock added editorial comment to his edition of John Wesley's *Journal*:

> It cannot be denied that from this time Wesley's views on ecclesiastical polity were slowly, perhaps, but seriously modified. He did not become a dissenter, nor did he lose his affection for the Church of England. Both his enemies and his admirers have quoted words and deeds of his, during the long transition period, that seem to justify the charge of inconsistency; but it was the inconsistency of a man emerging out of darkness into light, and who saw men as trees walking.[14]

Rack, adding to the discussion, suggested:

> It was, rather, a handy confirmation for defending a position into which he had been forced by events, experiences and very probably a 'providential' sense of a special call which had been developing during the past few years.[15]

Dr Rack continued to observe that Wesley's seizing upon and partly misinterpreting King suggested that he felt that he needed respectable authority to back a position forced upon him by Gospel imperatives.[16]

A further work to which John Wesley attributed great influence was Edward Stillingfleet's *Irenicum*, published in 1661.[17] Stillingfleet was an English divine born at Cranbourne, Dorset. In 1653 he was made a fellow of St John's college, Cambridge; later he became Vicar of Sutton, Bedfordshire, and then, in 1689, was consecrated Bishop of Worcester.

Stillingfleet wrote his *Irenicum* in an attempt to show that neither Christ nor the apostles left any precise instructions concerning the form of church government. Stillingfleet suggested that a compromise between the practice of the established church and the presbyterian model ought to be adopted. Thompson has told that Stillingfleet repented some 'injudicious expressions' in his *Irenicum*, but he never recanted its main theme. Indeed, 'he could not, without withdrawing and repudiating the entire book.'[18]

One of the earliest indications of John Wesley having read Stillingfleet can be found in his letter to Charles Wesley on 16 July 1755.[19] Through the influence of Stillingfleet, John Wesley came to understand that, whilst still preferring the episcopal order of church government, there could be no grounds for believing it to be scripturally prescribed, although, equally, there is nothing in scripture which

---

14   Curnock, *Journal*, 3:229.
15   Henry Rack, *Reasonable Enthusiast*, 295.
16   Henry Rack, *Reasonable Enthusiast*, 295.
17   Edward Stillingfleet (1635–99), *Irenicum*, (London, 1661).
18   Edgar W. Thompson, *Wesley: Apostolic Man*, 17.
19   Telford, *Letters*, 3:135. To Charles Wesley, 16 July 1755.

would refute the model. Stillingfleet, like King, argued that presbyters had an inherent right to ordain, and went further than King in asserting that ancient presbyters did in fact exercise this right in cases of necessity. Stillingfleet cited the precedent of the ancient church of Alexandria, where (according to Jerome) bishops were elevated and ordained by the presbyters, without the assistance of other bishops.

Stillingfleet was writing in the context of the conflicts over church order in the 1660s and the policy of 'comprehension'. He emphasised that all three main traditions had some justification in the New Testament and that none had been prescribed as of divine ordinance. Wesley took from Stillingfleet what he wanted for his own purposes. He claimed that Stillingfleet had convinced him that apostolic succession was not true, that those who were not ordained could preach, that as a presbyter he had the right to ordain, and that such ordinations did not entail separation from the Church of England.

Wesley did not state that his reading of King convinced him of his right to ordain. King's work would not support such an assertion. While allowing that bishop and presbyter were of the same order originally, King emphasised that the presbyter was still subject to the bishop as his agent.

John Wesley selected his evidence according to the result he was pursuing. He did not acknowledge Jeremy Taylor's work, which would have offered a contrary view:

> Imposition of hands is a duty and office necessary for the perpetuating of a church ... 'lest it expire in one age'. This power of imposition of hands for ordination is fixed upon the apostle and apostolic men, and not communicated to the seventy-two disciples or presbyters; for the apostles and apostolic men did so de facto, and were commanded to do so, and the seventy-two never did so. Therefore this office and ministry of the apostolate is distinct and superior to that of presbyters; and this distinction must be so continued to all ages of the church; for the thing was not temporary, but productive of an issue and succession, and therefore as perpetual as the clergy, as the church itself.[20]

John Wesley's encounters with the work of King and Stillingfleet signal the point of change in the public expression of his views. He came to reject the notion of the historic episcopate being the exclusive channel by which grace was conveyed to the church. Following King, Wesley believed that as a presbyter he was essentially of the same order as a bishop their difference being one of function. The Church of England understood the difference as being both of order and function.

John Wesley recognised that he was fulfilling an episcopal role in his oversight and government of the people called Methodists and in the direction of the Assistants. He was exercising an episcopal function. It is important, then, to realise

---

20   Jeremy Taylor, Bishop of Down and Connor, (1613–67) – *Episcopacy Asserted*, in *Works*, C.P. Eden (ed.), (London, 1849), 5:27 in G.R. Evans and J. Robert Wright, *The Anglican Tradition: A Handbook of Sources*, (London: SPCK/Minneapolis: Fortress, 1991), 213.

that John Wesley did not reject the episcopal system of church government, he merely adapted it for his own use. He believed himself engaged in an episcopal ministry. He took his model of church government from the established Church of England, but realigned it to his own purposes.

Nevertheless, John Wesley was out of order and reaching beyond his authority as a presbyter in the Church of England. King and Stillingfleet's arguments, no matter how Wesley used them, could not stand against the fact that a presbyter in that Church had no right to ordain at all.

John Wesley's claim that he could ordain, if he had to, was based on very selective early precedents chosen by himself. Furthermore, he had by this time proclaimed the principle by which all considerations of order were subordinated to Gospel priorities; a position which he was to hold for the rest of his life. He would avoid secession as long as he could, for the good of Methodism. He would only exercise his supposed powers when the Gospel, and the maintenance of Methodist integrity, demanded it. John Wesley believed that even if he did exercise his 'right' he would still not be separating from the church, according to his own convenient definition.

Wesley's understanding and interpretation of the teaching of scripture and tradition was another constraint which had a great influence upon him. Although at various points Wesley was obviously influenced by the conventions of the established church (as in the form of his later ordinations), he could manipulate these and the church Fathers to suit his purpose; they were apologetic devices rather than motives for action. Rack has commented that John Wesley 'used precedent to clothe the nakedness of his own will, seen by signs following the providential will of God for his own mission.'[21]

---

21   Henry Rack, *Reasonable Enthusiast*, 296.

Chapter 5

Ordination of the Assistants
Is it Separation from the Church of England?

John Wesley spent the large proportion of his life claiming loyalty to the Church of England, and avoiding separation from it. He knew that to ordain Methodist Assistants and preachers was tantamount to declaring himself, and his Connexion, separated. Despite this, John Wesley was, at times, tempted to ordain his people and take that step beyond the boundaries of the established church. Charles Wesley worried that his brother was, on occasion, too enthusiastic on the question of ordination and separation.

Discussing the issue of separation from the Church, Henry Rack has recounted a conversation between John Wesley and his brother which was precipitated by a friendly clergyman giving the sacrament of the Lord's Supper to some of the Methodists:

> In October 1754 Charles Wesley recorded that Charles Perronet (the son of the vicar of Shoreham) 'Gave the sacrament to the preachers Walsh and Deaves and then to twelve at Sister Garer's.' To this, he claimed, John only said: 'We have in effect ordained already.' He urged me to sign the preachers' certificates, was inclined to lay on hands,' and let the preachers administer.' A few days later: 'he is wavering; but willing to wait before he ordains or separates.' Other preachers had administered, and Charles wrote bitterly to a friend that 'since the Melchisedechians have been taken in, I have been excluded this cabinet council.' John was only thinking ordination not expedient rather than unlawful, and the rebel preachers were urging that he might ordain without separation. Charles pictured an unscrupulous cabal plotting against the church and for a separation through ordinations by his brother, who he saw as fatally weak-willed. He busied himself in drumming up support for a rival pressure-group and enlisted Grimshaw, who threatened to leave the Methodists if they allowed the preachers to administer communion.[1]

Charles Wesley's record of his brother's comment, concerning having in effect already ordained his preachers, is problematic. Assuming Charles was accurate in his reporting, the comment would appear to be entirely out of character with all that John Wesley was doing and saying in the 1750s. There is no supplementary evidence to support Charles Wesley's apparent belief that his brother John was, at this time, considering ordaining any of those in Connexion with him.

Whether lawful or not, John Wesley did not regard it as expedient to ordain at this early point. He considered himself still a loyal member and priest of the

---

1   Henry Rack, *Reasonable Enthusiast*, 297.

Church of England; he again declared that he had no intention of separating from the Church. Writing to Samuel Walker, curate at Truro, on 24 September 1755, Wesley said:

> At present I apprehend those, and those only, to separate from the Church who either renounce her fundamental doctrines or refuse to join in her public worship. As yet we have done neither; nor have we taken one step farther than we were convinced was our bounden duty. It is from a full conviction of this that we have (1) preached abroad, (2) prayed extempore, (3) formed societies, and (4) permitted preachers who were not episcopally ordained. And were we pushed on this side, were there no alternative allowed, we should judge it our bounden duty rather wholly to separate from the Church than to give up any one of these points. Therefore, if we cannot stop a separation without stopping lay preachers, the case is clear – we cannot stop it at all.

> 'But if we permit them, should we not do more? Should we not appoint them rather? since the bare permission puts the matter quite out of all our hands and deprived us of our influence.' In great measure it does; therefore to appoint them is far more expedient, if it be lawful. But is it lawful for presbyters circumstanced as we are to appoint other ministers? This is the very point wherein we desire advice, being afraid of leaning to our own understanding.

> It is undoubtedly 'needful,' as you observe, 'to come to some resolution in this point;' and the sooner the better. I therefore rejoice to hear that you think 'this matter may be better and more inoffensively ordered; and that a method may be found which, conducted with prudence and patience, will reduce the constitution of Methodism to due order, and render the Methodists under God more instrumental to the ends of practical religion.'[2]

A month later, 31 October 1755, John Wesley wrote in similar style to Thomas Adam. It would be wrong, he said, to separate from the established church and no action taken by the Methodists thus far could make separation either necessary or desirable. Continuing:

> We are fully convinced that to separate from an Established Church is never lawful but when it is absolutely necessary; and we do not see any such necessity yet. Therefore we have at present no thoughts of separation.

> With regard to the steps we have hitherto taken, we have used all the caution which was possible. We have done nothing rashly, nothing without deep and long consideration, hearing and weighing all objections, and much prayer. Nor have we taken one deliberate step of which we as yet see reason to repent. It is true in some things we vary from the rules of our Church; but no farther than we apprehend is our bounden duty. It is upon a full conviction of this that we preach abroad, use extempore prayer, form those who appear to be awakened into societies, and permit laymen whom we believe God has called to preach.

---

2   Baker, *Letters 1*, 2:595 and Telford, *Letters*, 3:146. To Samuel Walker, 24 September 1755.

I say permit, because we ourselves have hitherto viewed it in no other light. This we are clearly satisfied we may do: that we may do more we are not satisfied. It is not clear to us that presbyters so circumstanced as we may appoint or ordain others, but it is that we may direct as well as suffer them to do what we conceive they are moved to by the Holy Ghost. It is true that in ordinary cases both an inward and an outward call are requisite. But we apprehend there is something far from ordinary in the present case. And upon the calmest view of things we think they who are only called of God and not of man have more right to preach than they who are only called of man and not of God. Now, that many of the clergy, though called of man, are not called of God to preach His gospel is undeniable, (1) because they themselves utterly disclaim, nay, and ridicule, the inward call; (2) because they do not know what the gospel is, of consequence they do not and cannot preach it.[3]

On 3 July 1756 John Wesley wrote to James Clark outlining his feelings about the order of the established church. He wrote that, after Stillingfleet, he no longer accepted episcopacy as prescribed in scripture. He accepted that the form of government was that as practised by the established church, but rejected the notion that the Bishop should exercise authority by divine right; the Bishop may well be wrong. He continued:

As to my own judgement, I still believe 'the Episcopal form of Church government to be both scriptural and apostolical': I mean, well agreeing with the practice and writings of the Apostles. But that it is prescribed in scripture I do not believe. This opinion (which I once heartily espoused) I have been heartily ashamed of ever since I read Dr. Stillingfleet's *Irenicum*. I think he has unanswerably proved that neither Christ nor His Apostles prescribed any particular form of Church government, and that the plea for the divine right of Episcopacy was never heard of in the primitive church.

But were it otherwise, I would still call these 'smaller matters than the love of God and mankind.' And could any man answer these questions – 'Dost thou believe in the Lord Jesus Christ, God over all, blessed for evermore?'[4]

On 3 September 1756 John Wesley wrote again to Samuel Walker outlining his evangelical motivation. The call to bring the light of the Gospel into the dark places of the land, by whatever means available to him, led him to adopt methods which the church regarded as unorthodox:

I have one point of view – to promote, so far as I am able, vital, practical religion; and by the grace of God to beget, preserve, and increase the life of God in the souls of men. On this single principle I have hitherto proceeded, and taken no step but in subserviency to it. With this view, when I found it absolutely necessary for the continuance of the work which God had begun in many souls (which their regular pastors generally used all possible means to destroy), I permitted several of their brethren, whom I believe God had called thereto and qualified for the work, to comfort, exhort, and instruct those who were athirst for God or who walked in the light of his countenance. But, as the persons

---

3   Baker, *Letters*, 2:609 and Telford, *Letters*, 3:149. To Thomas Adam, 31 October 1755. Original italics.

4   Telford, *Letters*, 3:182. To James Clark, 3 July 1756.

so qualified were few and those who wanted their assistance very many, it followed that most of these were obliged to travel continually from place to place; and this occasioned several regulations from time to time, which were chiefly made in our Conferences.

So great a blessing has from the beginning attended the labours of itinerants, that we have been more and more convinced every year of the more than lawfulness of this proceeding. And the inconveniences, most of which we foresaw from the very first, have been both fewer and smaller than were expected. Rarely two in one year out of the whole number of preachers have either separated themselves or been rejected by us. A great majority have all along behaved as becometh the gospel of Christ, and I am clearly persuaded still desire nothing more than to spend and be spent for their brethren ...

Your last advice is, 'That as many of our preachers as are fit for it be ordained, and that the others be fixed to certain societies, not as preachers, but as readers or inspectors ...' But is that which you propose a better way? This should be cooly and calmly considered.[5]

In his *A Roman Catechism, with a reply thereto (1756)*, John Wesley rejected the notion that ordination itself was a sacrament.[6] Writing:

Q. 85. Is ordination a sacrament?
A. It is truly and properly a sacrament, and doth confer grace; and whoso denies this, is accursed. (Concil. Trid. Sess. 7, Can. 1,23, cap.3, Can.3.)

Reply. We account ordination to be of divine institution, and that by it a ministerial commission is conveyed; but how necessary soever this office is to the Church, and grace for the exercise of it, yet as that grace is not promised to it, we cannot admit it to be properly and truly a sacrament.[7]

It has been shown that John Wesley's view of ordination centred upon its being the means of commissioning his preachers to administer the sacraments. Such a view can confirm the assertion that John Wesley's understanding of the purpose of ordination remained consistent with his upbringing and churchmanship. However, in his *Reply to the Roman Catechism* Wesley rejected the notion that ordination itself was a sacrament. He stated that ordination implies the conveyance of a ministerial commission, not the transmission of grace. Furthermore, Wesley rejected the concept of a mediatorial priesthood and denied the right of the priest to absolve sins. Such a position reduced the act of ordination from an ontological action of God in which the church participates, to an authority-giving functional action of the church. It can, therefore, be suggested that whilst John Wesley's view of the purpose of ordination remained consistent with his upbringing and churchmanship, his views on the nature of that ordination underwent radical and dramatic modification.

---

5   Telford, *Letters*, 3:192–4. 'To Samuel Walker', 3 September 1756.
6   Jackson, *Works*, 10:126–7. This work is actually a reprint of a work by John Williams (1582-1650), Archbishop of York (1641); see Frank Baker, *John Wesley and the Church of England*, 132.
7   Jackson, *Works*, 10:126.

Ordination remained, in John Wesley's understanding, the means by which authority to perform a sacramental ministry was granted to individuals. He believed ordination to be an authority-giving, rather than a grace-imparting, rite. Furthermore, the authority vested in the rite was understood in terms of human institutional authority. If he were to ordain his preachers, then he would have been granting them his authority, just as he had given them his authority to preach, only for so long as they remained in Connexion with him.

The authority granted by Wesley to those who worked with him was dependent upon their relationship with him. John Wesley, the founder of the Methodist movement, was acting as the scriptural *episcopos* of the movement, directing the functions and places of work of those who assisted him. One hears echoes of Cyprian, 'hence you know that the Bishop is in the Church and the Church in the Bishop, and if any one be not with the Bishop he is not in the Church.'[8]

The Methodists were personally responsible to John Wesley alone. Although there were to regard themselves as faithful members of the Church of England, they were not under the authority of any establishment Bishop. The Church of England did not recognise them as lay preachers and so could exercise no authority over them. Wesley maintained a rigid discipline over his workers; he alone appointed them and directed their work. They were forbidden to engage in trades or publish work without his permission; they could not attend the Conference unless expressly invited to do so. When the autocratic nature of John Wesley's oversight was challenged he explained his viewpoint to the Conference. He believed that he had the right to exercise power over the people who were in Connexion with him; they joined him freely and, if they did not agree with him, they were free to leave at their own discretion.[9]

John Wesley's conventional attitude regarded ordination as the only acceptable means of authorisation for a sacramental ministry. But he had no intention for his preachers to expand their work beyond that of proclaiming the Gospel. His intention, when separating the Assistants and Preachers, was that they were being set apart for the work of preaching. It was this intention which was all important in understanding the mind of John Wesley on the matter. The entries in Charles Wesley's Journal for 19 and 24 October 1745 make it clear that John Wesley, up to that point, had not ordained, nor intended ordination of any of his people:

> I was with my brother, who said nothing of Perronet, except 'We have in effect ordained already.' He urged me to sign the preachers' certificates; was inclined to lay on hands and let the preachers administer … Was with my brother. He is wavering; but willing to wait before he ordains or separates.[10]

---

8   Cyprian, *Ep. lxvi.7,* and see discussion above, 10.
9   *Minutes,* 1766, 1.60.
10   Luke Tyerman, *Life and Times of John Wesley,* 3 vols, (London: Hodder and Stoughton, 1870–1), 2:202 and Frank Baker, *Charles Wesley as revealed by his letters,* (London: Epworth, 1948), 92.

The comment stated clearly that John Wesley believed that even though he may have in effect already ordained, he did not intend that he had in fact ordained his preachers. He authorised and appointed his preachers to preach only; he had not ordained them. Without that ordination, he believed, it was quite wrong for his preachers to administer the sacrament of the Lord's Supper. However, some of the preachers took it upon themselves to administer the sacraments at the meetings of the Methodist societies. Gunter has commented that John Wesley continually faced the difficulty that many of those associated with him 'either did not understand his functional ecclesiological dialectic or simply refused to accept it.'[11]

In the early 1750s, some of the preachers had themselves licensed as Dissenting Preachers according to the requirements of the Act of Toleration. Such men as Charles and Edward Perronet and Thomas Walsh, having been licensed, began to administer the Lord's Supper, without the permission of John Wesley. These preachers were not ignorant, but were men of high standing and great influence who were, in the opinion of Luke Tyerman, as capable of forming correct opinions as were the Wesleys:

> They had a right to be heard; and it was hardly fair to denounce them because they thought that the Methodists were entitled to the sacraments of the Christian Church; and that they, as divinely called preachers of Christ's religion, might be permitted to administer ordinances which that religion solemnly enjoined.[12]

In a letter dated 8 October 1755, John Wesley advised Paul Greenwood that:

> Unless there should be a very particular call, you should not act publicly til you are ordained. Give yourself to reading, meditation, prayer; and do all the good you can in a private manner. Pride and impetuosity of temper will be apt to lead you out of the way.[13]

That John Wesley's pattern of ministry evolved over a period of time, rather than exhibiting planned development, lay him open to the charge of inconsistency. In a letter to Nicholas Norton, 3 September 1756, Wesley replied to the charge:

> I act on one and the same principle still. My principle (frequently declared) is this: 'I submit to every ordinance of man wherever I do conceive there is an absolute necessity for acting contrary to it.' Consistently with this I do tolerate lay preaching, because I conceive there is an absolute necessity for it; in as much as were it not, thousands of souls would perish everlastingly. Yet I do not tolerate lay-administering, because I do not conceive there is any such necessity for it; seeing it does not appear that, if this is not all, one soul will perish for the want of it.
>
> I am therefore, so far from self-inconsistency in tolerating the former and not the latter, that I really should be self-inconsistent were I to act otherwise: were I to break, or allow

---

11   W. Stephen Gunter, *The Limits of 'Love Divine'*, 161.

12   Luke Tyerman, *Life and Times of John Wesley*, 2:200.

13   Baker, *Letters*, 26:601 and Telford, *Letters*, 3:147. 'To Paul Greenwood', 8 October 1755.

others to break, an ordinance of man, where there is no necessity, I should contradict my own principle as much as if I did not allow it to be broken where there is.[14]

In February 1760 some of the Methodists at Norwich, including Paul Greenwood, John Murlin and Thomas Mitchell, took it upon themselves to get themselves licensed as Dissenting Preachers and to administer the Lord's Supper. Charles Wesley was convinced that this was the final event which would lead to Methodism separating from the Church of England. Charles Wesley wrote to his brother, who was in Ireland at the time:

> We are come to the Rubicon. Shall we pass or shall we not? ... Three Preachers, whom we thought we could have depended upon, have taken upon them to administer the sacrament, without any ordination, and without acquainting us (or even yourself) of it beforehand ... That the rest will soon follow their example I believe; because 1. They think they may do it with impunity. 2. Because a large majority imagine they have a right, as Preachers, to administer the sacraments. So long ago as the Conference at Leeds, I took down their names. 3. Because they have betrayed an impatience to separate ... upon the whole, I am fully persuaded almost all our Preachers are corrupted already ... You must wink very hard not to see all this. You have connived at it too, too long. But I now call upon you to consider with me what is to be done; first to prevent a separation; secondly, to save the few uncorrupted Preachers; thirdly, to make the best of those that are corrupted.[15]

In response to his brother's concern, John Wesley suggested Charles investigate the matter at Norwich. Charles agreed to do this task, on condition that John give him a letter condemning those who had been involved. Despite this, Charles remained aggrieved that his brother only gently rebuked the miscreants at Norwich, preferring to leave the matter to the following Conference. Charles wrote to William Grimshaw, Vicar of Haworth, one of the Church of England clergymen who were sympathetic to Methodism:

> Three of our steadiest Preachers give the sacrament at Norwich, with no other ordination or authority than a sixpenny license. My brother approves of it. All the rest will probably follow their example. What then must be the consequence? Not only separation, but general confusion, and the destruction of the work, so far as it depends on the Methodists ... I cannot get leave of my conscience, to do nothing in the meantime towards guarding our children against the approaching evil ... I am convinced things are come to a crisis. We must now resolve either to separate from the Church, or to continue in it the rest of our days.[16]

---

14   Telford, *Letters*, 3:186. 'To Nicholas Norton', 3 September 1756.

15   Thomas Jackson, *Life of Charles Wesley, M.A.* 2 vols, (London: John Mason, 1841) 2:180–1, 'Letter to John Wesley,' March 1760.

16   'Letter to Rev. Mr. Grimshaw,' 27 March 1760 in Frank Baker, *William Grimshaw, 1708–63*, (London: Epworth, 1963), 252–5. The sixpenny license reference concerns the registration of the Preachers as Dissenters under the terms of the Act of Toleration.

Grimshaw responded with the sort of sentiments that Charles Wesley wanted to hear:

> The licensing of Preachers and Preaching Houses is a matter that I never expected to have seen or hard among the Methodists. If I had, I dare say, I had never entered into connection with them. I desire to continue; but how can I do it consistently with my Relation to the Church of England? ... The Methodists are no longer Members of the Church of England: They are as really a Body of Dissenters from her as the Presbyterians, Baptists, Quakers or Independents. How have I complained of this all that winter! ... I little thought your brother approved ... these things, especially at the Preachers' doings at Norwich. If it be so ... It is time for me to shift for myself – to disown all connection with the Methodists – to stay at home and take care of my Parish ... I hereby henceforth assure you that I disclaim all farther and future connection with the Methodists. I shall quietly ... retire without Noise or Tumult. In general, as the Licensing of Preachers and Places I know no expedient to prevent it. The thing is gone too far; it has become inveterate ... Even while you live the licensed Preachers, tho' they continue with you, will do worse than this after your Death. For now even upon their six-penny License they dare themselves to administer Sacraments; whereas then they will qualify themselves for it by obtaining Presbyterian ordination. Dissenters the Methodists will all shortly be. I am fully satisfied it cannot be prevented.[17]

Charles Wesley read Grimshaw's letter to the London Society, inciting a great deal of support in his favour. Charles Wesley remarked in a letter to his wife:

> All cried out against the licensed Preachers ... They all cried out that they would answer for ninety-nine out of a hundred in London that they would live and die in the church.[18]

The issue was dealt with by the Conference, meeting at Bristol in August 1760. It seems that the only record of the event is that of Howell Harris:

> [Aug. 29, 1760] ... Mr. John Wesley shewed from the practice of the Church of England, the Kirk of Scotland, Calvinists and Lutherans and the Primitive Churches, that they all made preaching or prophesying or evangelising and administering the ordinances two distinct offices. When they proposed to him to ordain them, he said it was not clear to him that he had a power to do so except they were wholly cut off from the Church by a public act, and also that it would be a total renouncing of the Bishops and the Established Church, which he could not do and stumbling thousands. Many spake well on the opposite side, shewing they were already dissented from the Church, and by their being ordained and licensed they would remove the prejudice of the Dissenters. If they were sent to preach, why not administer the sacraments? ... Mr. John and Charles Wesley spake their opinion strong of the unlawfulness of a layman administering the ordinances.

---

17   'Letter from Mr. Grimshaw,' 31 March 1760. Cited by Baker, *William Grimshaw*, 255–7 and Jackson, *Life of Charles Wesley*, 2:189–90.
18   'Letter to Mrs. Charles Wesley,' 13 April 1760. Cited by Baker, *Charles Wesley*, 102–3.

[Aug.30] Sure the Lord has made a stand against the breach going to be made in the work by introducing licensing and even ordination, and so a total separation from the Church. Charles and I were the rough workers, and John more meekly, and said he could not ordain, and said if he was not ordained he would look upon it as murder if he gave the ordinances. He struck dumb the reasoners by saying he would renounce them in a quarter of an hour, that they were the most foolish and ignorant in the whole Conference.[19]

At the same time as some of Wesley's preachers were entering into relationships with the Dissenters, he was making provision for others of their number to enter in the orders of the Church of England. One imagines that this was the pinnacle of John Wesley's ambition. He aimed at enlivening the work of that Church; what better way than to be able to supply it with ministers from among the ranks of the Methodist societies? On 3 May 1758, John Wesley wrote to Samuel Furly concerning the possibility of obtaining ordination into Anglican orders:

Two conversations I have had with the Bishop of Londonderry, and *processimus pulchre*. I intend to write to him in a few days, and then I shall be able to form a better judgement. He loves the Methodists from his heart, but he is not free from the fear of man. Yet I have much hope that love will conquer fear.[20]

It is also known that John Wesley arranged for Thomas Maxfield to be ordained into Anglican orders by Dr William Barnard,[21] a close friend of the Countess of Huntingdon, who in 1747 had become the Bishop of Londonderry. Etheridge has written of Maxfield's ordination:

He had been ordained by the Bishop of Londonderry, not only for the sake of giving a man of ardent zeal and extraordinary talent a defined status in the Church, but more especially as a mark of the prelate's great esteem for the Founder of Methodism. 'Remember,' said he, 'I ordain you as a helper of Mr. Wesley, that that good man may not work himself to death.'[22]

John Wesley's *Journal* entry for 23 April 1763, after Maxfield had separated himself from Methodism, records:

---

19   Tom Benyon, ed, *Howell Harris, Reformer and Soldier,* (Caernarfon: Calvinistic Methodist Bookroom, 1958), 80–2.

20   Telford, *Letters,* 4:19. To Samuel Furly, 3 May 1758 ('*processimus pulchre*' 'We made good progress') and compare with the letter from Wesley to Furly 1 April 1758 in which he says 'Very probably I may procure your admission into orders ...' Telford, *Letters,* 4:14.

21   Dr William Barnard (c. 1697–1768) had become Bishop of Derry in 1747 after being Chaplain to the King (1728), Vicar of St Bride's, Fleet Street (1729–47), a position held simultaneously with being Dean of Rochester (1743), and Bishop of Raphoe (1744).

22   J.W. Etheridge, *The Life of the Rev. Thomas Coke, D.C.L.,* (London: John Mason, 1860), 31–2.

He was by me (by those who did it at my insistence) recommended to the Bishop of Derry to be ordained priest, who told him then (I had it from his own mouth), 'Mr.Maxfield, I ordain you to assist that good man, that he may not work himself to death.'[23]

We can understand John Wesley's motive for obtaining ordination for his associates from the hand of bona fide Anglican Bishops. If indeed, as we have asserted, the Assistants were meant to be interim, extraordinary, ministers for the purpose of stirring-up the ordinary ministers, then it would be a major advance to arrange for entry into orders of the more able of them. John Wesley's aim was the raising up of the Church of England; the entry into orders of his Assistants would be entirely consistent with this aim.

Less clear, either then or now, was John Wesley's motive for getting involved, in the early 1760s, with Erasmus, the putative Greek Bishop. There were questions at the time about the authenticity of Erasmus's position. Tyerman has told that John Jones wrote to the patriarch of Smyrna and received confirmation that Erasmus was indeed Bishop of Arcadia, in Crete.[24] However, in March 1764, B. Richards wrote to Charles Wesley suggesting the possibility that Erasmus was a fraud – after all the 'Bishop' may have left his homeland because of crime or misbehaviour. He further suggested that anyone ordained by Erasmus may be liable to prosecution in the Ecclesiastical court. Charles Wesley called him 'a wizard' and Vincent Perronet declared the wish that 'his Grecian Lordship had been preaching either in Lapland or Japan.'[25]

According to the evangelical clergyman, Augustus Toplady, author of the hymn *Rock of Ages*, writing in 1771, it appears that the chaplain to the Greeks in Amsterdam held Erasmus to have been an impostor. He further suggested that, having seen one of the ordination certificates issued by Erasmus, it was written in ancient Greek rather than the modern which was used by the church of which he claimed to be Bishop.[26]

George Tsoumas, investigating the character concluded that 'Erasmus was not a canonical Bishop of the Greek Orthodox Church.' He has suggested four reasons for his conclusion. Firstly, Erasmus exhibited total ignorance of the practice, customs and laws of the Church he was supposed to represent. Secondly, the ordination certificate did not match that of the Greek Orthodox Church of the period. Thirdly, he was destitute, a Greek Bishop would not have been so. Fourthly, he was not listed in the catalogues of the Bishops of Crete.[27]

---

23   Curnock, *Journal*, 5:11 and W. Reginald Ward and Richard P. Heitzenrater (eds), *Journal and Diaries*, 21:409.

24   Luke Tyerman, *Life and Time of John Wesley*, 2:486.

25   A. B. Sackett, *John Wesley and the Greek Orthodox Bishop*, in *Proceedings* of the Wesley Historical Society, 38 (1972): 83.

26   A. B. Sackett, *John Wesley and the Greek Orthodox Bishop*, 86, quoting from Toplady's *Works*, 5:337.

27   George Tsoumas, *The Greek Orthodox Theological Review*, II:2 (1956): 62–73.

A.B. Sackett, reviewing the material and circumstances relating to the incident, was not so confident to reject the Bishop's authenticity. Rather, he rejected some of the assertions made about the Bishop, particularly those of Toplady.[28] Sackett asserted that Gerasimos Avlonites of Arkadia would have been a resident of the monastery south of Rethymon in central Crete. This place was a centre of resistance to foreign domination so he had probably been driven into exile around 1739 by the oppressive Turkish régime. The Greeks in Amsterdam, rather than denounce him as an imposture, acknowledged him as founding the first Greek Church there. He was not an ignorant man, but a renowned scholar, having participated in the publication of a serious work in London and Amsterdam. That the Bishop accepted fees for the ordination was acceptable, for his church was impoverished, 'From patriarchs downwards, all paid for their offices.'[29]

Sackett, whilst acknowledging that the name of Gerasimos Avlonites does not appear in the present list of Bishops of the fortress-monastery of Arkadia, recognised that the eighteenth century was the 'dark-ages' of Cretan history. He stated that there are large gaps in the records even of those places of which much is known. It is quite likely that many more names have been lost, 'of exiles escaping from Turkish or Church authorities, or resisters or schismatics, or of good men who have left no memorial.'[30]

Somewhat colourfully, Sackett concluded, as probably one must, that:

> it would seem that in the absence of decisive record in Crete, the most satisfactory and safest thing – the most probably accurate – is to take at his word this needy, meteoric ecclesiastical wanderer exiled from home and become in his own words and those of the psalmist before him like 'a pelican in the wilderness, an owl of the waste places, a sparrow upon the house-top.'[31]

John Wesley, believing Erasmus genuine, requested that he ordain John Jones, who had been one of his Assistants for seventeen years and was regarded by Wesley as 'a man well versed both in the languages and other parts of learning.'[32] But, what was the purpose of this? Presumably Wesley believed that such ordination would be acceptable to the establishment as being episcopal ordination. Maybe it would have been acceptable as episcopal ordination, but it was still not ordination into Anglican orders and would surely not have been regarded with great favour by John Wesley's adversaries.

In the early 1760s some of Wesley's preachers, acting on their own behalf, without the direction of Wesley, secured ordination by the hand of Erasmus. John Telford's editorial comment in his edition of John Wesley's *Letters* suggested that

---

28   A.B. Sackett, *John Wesley and the Greek Orthodox Bishop*, 99.

29   A.B. Sackett, *John Wesley and the Greek Orthodox Bishop*, 100–1.

30   A.B. Sackett, *John Wesley and the Greek Orthodox Bishop*, 102.

31   A.B. Sackett, *John Wesley and the Greek Orthodox Bishop*, 102.

32   Telford, *Letters*, 4:290. To the printers of *The St. James Chronicle*, 10 February 1765.

Thomas Bryant had been ordained by Erasmus in 1760.[33] One could well ask, though, why it took John Wesley until January 1765 to deal with this issue. The motivating force would seem to have been that the event became public knowledge and it therefore became necessary for John Wesley to be seen to discipline those who had been involved.

Telford has reported that John Wesley was forced into dealing with the matter after the names of the six Methodists involved in the ordination had been published in *Lloyd's Evening News*. The Rev. Messrs. Madan, Romaine and Shirley required Wesley to bring charges against the group for having bought an ordination in a foreign tongue.[34] On 7 January 1765 John Wesley called a Conference at the Foundery in order to deal with the matter. Some days later, he reported the result of the meeting to his brother Charles, who we can imagine would have been unhappy about the ordinations:

On Monday morning I desired the preachers and the stewards to meet me. It was then inquired, –

1. Can James Thwaite, B. Russen, Rd. Perry, James Satles, John Oliver, and T. Bryant, who have bought an ordination in an unknown tongue, be received by us as clergymen? No.

2. Can we receive them any longer as preachers? No.

3. Can we receive them as members of our Society? No.

And this I ordered to be signified to each of them immediately.[35]

On 12 and 29 January 1765 the St. James's Chronicle published letters concerning the ordinations of the Methodists by the Greek Bishop. Replying to the Chronicle, on 5 February 1765, Wesley wrote:

To the four questions proposed to me in your last week's paper, I answer: –

(1) None of those six persons lately ordained by a Greek Bishop were ordained with my consent or knowledge.

(2) I will not, cannot, own or receive them as clergymen.

(3) I think an ordination performed in a language not understood by the persons ordained is not valid.

(4) I think it is absolutely unlawful for any one to give money to the Bishop (or to any one for him) for ordaining him.[36]

---

33   Telford, *Letters*, 4:252. Introductory comment on John Wesley's letter to Sarah Moore, 5 July 1764.

34   Telford, *Letters*, 4:290–1.

35   Telford, *Letters*, 4:287–8. To the Revd. Charles Wesley, 11 January 1765.

36   Telford, *Letters*, 4:288–9. To the printers of *The St. James Chronicle*, 5 February 1765.

In a further letter to the *Chronicle*, dated 10 February 1765, John Wesley recounted how Bishop Erasmus came to be amongst the Methodists:

> A year or two ago I found a stranger perishing for want and expecting daily to be thrown in prison. He told me he was a Greek Bishop. I examined his credentials, and was fully satisfied. After much conversation (in Latin and Greek, for he spoke no English at all) I determined to relieve him effectively; which I did without delay, and promised to send him back to Amsterdam, where he had several friends of his own nation. And this I did, without any farther view, merely upon motives of humanity. After this he ordained Mr. John Jones, a man well versed in both the languages and other parts of learning.

> When I was gone out of town, Bishop Erasmus was prevailed upon to ordain Lawrence Coughlan, a person who had no learning at all.

> Some time after, Mr. Maxfield, or his friends, sent for him from Amsterdam, to ordain Mr. S____t and three other persons, as unlearned as any of the Apostles, but I believe not so much inspired.

> In December last year he was sent for again, and ordained six other persons, members of our Society, but in every way, I think, unqualified for that office. These I judged it my duty to disclaim (to waive all other considerations) for a fault which I know not who can excuse, buying an ordination in an unknown tongue.[37]

The offenders were removed from the Methodist Society. John Wesley wrote to them on 27 February 1765, but one gets the feeling that he was not over-concerned about the issue:

> Mr. Madan, Mr, Romaine, and the good-natured Mr. Shirley are almost out of patience with me for not disowning you on the house-top. In this situation of things it would be utter madness in me to do anything which they would call contumacy. I am every way bound to my good behaviour, and obliged to move with all possible circumspection. Were I to allow your preaching now, I should be in a hotter fire than ever. That you will preach again by-and-by I doubt not; but it is certain the time is not come yet.[38]

Lawson has commented that:

> All that remains to be said about the Greek ordinations is that they could be considered valid, but because they were conferred in England by a foreign prelate they are bound to be regarded as irregular.[39]

The occurrence illustrates that John Wesley did not regard ordination as having a mechanical validity dependent simply upon the right actions and words. It is clear that he held firm to the necessity for the act to be in accord with the expression of the Church's will. Whilst the ordinations may have been technically correct and valid, they held no such validity as either orders of the Church of England or of

---

37   Telford, *Letters*, 4:289. To the printers of *The St. James Chronicle*, 10 February 1765.

38   Telford, *Letters*, 4:291.

39   A.B. Lawson, *John Wesley and the Christian Ministry: The sources and development of his opinions and practice.* (London: SPCK, 1963), 124.

any equivalent office amongst the Methodist societies. The authority to act as ordained Methodist Assistants was not conveyed by the Greek ordination.

Charles Wesley's opposition to the separation from the Church, lay administration of the sacraments and ordination of the Methodists was almost hysterical. He was frightened that John had secretly encouraged the movements. Following the incident with Bishop Erasmus one can see that the fears were probably well-founded. Jackson wrote of Charles Wesley that:

> He even suggested that these preachers might have obtained ordination by the imposition of John's hands ... for he had by implication avowed his right to ordain: having many years ago published to the world his conviction, that in the apostolic church, Bishops and Presbyters were of the same order.[40]

Gunter has recounted that Charles Wesley expressed his fears to Walter Sellon, a former Methodist preacher and Master of Kingswood School. Sellon had, upon recommendation of the Countess of Huntingdon, received Episcopal ordination and had been made Vicar of Smithsby, near Ashby-de-la-Zouch, Leicestershire. Charles asked Sellon to write to John Wesley and urge him to moderation in his views on the administration of the sacraments and on faithfulness to the Church of England. Later, Charles urged Sellon to again write to John Wesley and encourage him to 'take the utmost pains to settle the preachers, discharging those who are irreclaimable, and never receiving another without this previous condition, that he shall never leave the Church.'[41]

After dealing with the Greek Bishop affair, a further nineteen years passed before John Wesley took matters concerning the ordination of Methodist preachers any further. It was in 1784 that Wesley determined not only to give some of them authority to administer the sacraments, but to give that authority formally by prayer and the laying on of hands. He was impelled towards this action by the irresistible force of circumstances.

In 1771 Francis Asbury had been sent by John Wesley to work amongst the Methodists in America. He had arrived in Philadelphia on 27 October 1771 as subordinate to Richard Boardman, Wesley's Assistant in the city. Although, initially, the American Methodists continued to look to John Wesley for leadership, Asbury began to take more and more work upon himself. By October 1772 Asbury had received a letter from Wesley appointing him as an Assistant.[42]

On his way to America, the twenty-six year old Asbury had written in his Journal that 'If God does not acknowledge me in America, I will soon return to

---

40   Thomas Jackson, *The life of the Rev. Charles Wesley, M.A., sometime Student of Christ Church, Oxford; comprising a review of his poetry, sketches of the rise and progress of Methodism, with notices of contemporary events and characters*, 2 vols, (London: John Mason, 1841), 2:70.

41   W. Stephen Gunter, *The Limits of 'Love Divine'*, 172 with quotation of letter from Jackson, *The life of the Rev. Charles Wesley*, 2:71.

42   Elmer T. Clark, J. Manning Potts, and Jacob S. Payton (eds), *The Journal and Letters of Francis Asbury*, 3 vols, (Nashville: Abingdon, 1958), 1:46.

England. I know my views are upright now; may they never be otherwise.'[43] The statement echoed John Wesley's own method of testing a ministry according to its fruit. Asbury believed that for him to be 'acknowledged' would be to see the fruit of renewed lives as the result of his ministry. That he received such acknowledgement is evident, he never returned to England and was described by one of his contemporaries as being 'Next to Mr. Wesley ... the most unwearied itinerant the world ever saw.'[44]

The American War of Independence was a period of difficulty for the Methodists, who were regarded as representatives of an English movement opposed to the revolution.[45] Although the majority of the Anglican clergy and Methodists Assistants had left America, Asbury remained in the country. Although he had managed to keep the Methodist movement alive, the end of the war did not though, bring an end to Asbury's difficulties.

The great problem for Christianity in the newly-independent America was the lack of ordained ministers. In 1784 there were 14998 Methodists being served by 83 non-ordained, itinerant Methodist Preachers. Furthermore, there were only a few Anglican priests and no Bishop in the new country.[46]

Some American Methodists called for a break away from John Wesley's leadership and, in May 1779, members of the Fluvanna Conference, in Virginia, instigated a movement for presbyteral ordination.[47] Going against the wishes of both Wesley and Asbury, the Assistants gathered together and ordained each other. Although the Methodists loyal to Wesley were dominant, it became clear that action had to be taken in order to prevent Asbury and Wesley losing control of the societies in America.

John Wesley was overwhelmed by the importance of responding to the need for ordained ministers in America. However, Dr Robert Lowth, the Bishop of London, who was technically responsible for all areas overseas, would not, or could not, in 1780, meet the need, refusing to allow Anglican ordinations to take place. The main difficulty was that the Church of England Ordinal made frequent references to ordination and appointment being according to the law, not only of the church, but also of the Realm. The rite also included a oath concerning Royal Sovereignty. Following the American War of Independence, use of such a liturgy for the setting apart of American clergy was at least inappropriate and possibly illegal.

---

43   Elmer T. Clark, J. Manning Potts, and Jacob S. Payton (eds), *The Journal and Letters of Francis Asbury*, 1:4.

44   Thomas Ware, *Sketches of the Life and Travels of Thomas Ware*, (New York: T. Mason and G. Lane, 1832), 184.

45   Wesley's pamphlet *A Calm Address to our American Colonies (1775)* restated the main arguments from Samuel Johnson's *Taxation not Tyranny*. A friend of the Methodists burned the shipment of pamphlets at New York Wharf.

46   Luke Tyerman, *Life and Times of the Rev. John Wesley*, 3:427.

47   See editor's note, Telford, *Letters*, 7:20.

John Wesley was not the only one to come up against this difficulty; the American Anglicans were trying to solve their own difficulties. Their story concerns the ordination of Dr Samuel Seabury as Bishop. Seabury was elected by a meeting of the Connecticut clergy to be consecrated as Bishop. He arrived in England in 1783, but the request was declined by the Archbishop of York (there being nobody in the post at Canterbury at that time) on the ground that an oath of allegiance to the English King was required from the would-be Bishop and could not be dispensed with apart from an Act of Parliament. Commenting that 'Nobody here will risk anything for the sake of the Church,'[48] Seabury turned to the Scottish Bishops, who were not subject to the same laws, and was consecrated by three of them on 14 November 1784.

Behind the story of Seabury's ordination lay a long record of inaction and rejection of the American problem by the Anglican authorities in England. Nearly forty years earlier, Archbishop John Potter had pressed for the claims of the American colonies to have a Bishop. His successor was indifferent to the need, and later efforts of Archbishop Secker were frustrated. At that time in the Anglican Church in America, no colonist could take holy orders without travelling to England for ordination. Edgar Thompson has recorded the indignation of the Americans, reproducing a letter but failing to identify either its source or destination:

> To this Church of England was our immediate application directed, earnestly requesting a Bishop to collect, govern and continue our scattered, wandering and sinking Church; and great was, and continues to be, our surprise that a request so reasonable in itself, so congruous to the nature and government of that Church, and begging for the appointments, so absolutely necessary in the Church of Christ as they and we believe a Bishop to be, should be refused. We hope that the successors of the Apostles in England have sufficient reasons to justify themselves to the world and to God. We, however, know of none such, nor can our imagination grant any.[49]

It was imperative to John Wesley that the case of America should be met. He discussed the situation with Thomas Coke and raised the possibility of ordaining Methodists for work in the new situation. The plan was that Wesley should ordain one, possibly Coke, to an episcopal function with the intention that that person had authority to ordain others to the Sacramental ministry in America. Coke, who was not so certain that such a move would be appropriate, wanted to travel to America and assess the situation before committing himself to such a radical plan. However, on 9 August 1784, Coke wrote to John Wesley:

> Honoured and dear Sir,
>
> The more maturely I consider the subject, the more expedient it seems to me that the power of ordaining others should be received by me from you, by the imposition of your

---

48   Frank Baker, *John Wesley and the Church of England*, 274.
49   Edgar W. Thompson, *Wesley: Apostolic Man*, 64.

hands; and that you should lay hands on Brother Whatcoat and Brother Vasey, for the following reasons:

1. It seems to me the most scriptural way, and most agreeable to the practice of the primitive churches. 2. I may want all the influence in America which you can throw into my scale. Mr. Brackenbury informed me at Leeds that he saw a letter in London from Mr. Asbury, in which he observed 'that he should not receive any person deputed by you to take any part of the superintendency of the work invested in him,' – or words that implied so much. I do not feel the least degree of prejudice in my mind against Mr. Asbury; on the contrary, a very great love and esteem; and I am determined not to stir a finger without his consent, unless sheer necessity obliges me; but rather to lie at his feet in all things. But as the journey is long, and you cannot spare me often, and it is well to provide against all events, and an authority formally received from you will be fully admitted by the people, and my exercising the office of ordination without that formal authority may be disputed, if there be any opposition on any other account; I could therefore earnestly wish you would exercise that power in this instance, which I have not the shadow of a doubt but God hath invested you with for the good of the Connexion. I think you have tried me too often to doubt whether I will in any degree use the power you are pleased to invest in me with further than I believe absolutely necessary for the prosperity of the work ... In short, it appears to me that everything should be prepared, and everything proper prepared, and everything proper to be done, that can possibly be done, this side of the water ...[50]

At the meeting of the Methodist Conference in August 1784 Thomas Vasey and Richard Whatcoat were chosen to accompany Coke to America, after first receiving diaconal and presbyteral ordination from the hand of Wesley. It would, though, be wrong to assume that John Wesley's plan was universally popular. A number of the Methodists were opposed to the scheme, as were many of the evangelical Anglican clergymen who, otherwise, were sympathetic to John Wesley, men such as John Fletcher and James Creighton.

Despite the criticism, it was on 1 September 1784, at Bristol, that John Wesley capitulated to necessity and, with the uneasy assistance of James Creighton, undertook the ordination of the Methodist preachers. It is believed that these ordinations took place at 6 Dighton Street, Bristol, the home of Mr J. Castleman. Coke, Whatcoat and Vasey arrived in Bristol, en route to America, on the evening before.

In John Wesley's account of the ordinations for America, one hears echoes of his earlier decision to take to the fields of Kingswood to preach the gospel, where men and women were dying in ignorance. This time the needy were identified as the desolate sheep of America. Where men and women were in such desolation, for the want of the sacraments, the conventions must yield and law must let him pass. In his *Journal* he wrote:

---

50   Henry Moore, *The life of the Rev. John Wesley, A.M.* 2 vols, (London: John Kershaw, 1825), 2:530.

Being now clear in my own mind, I took a step which I had long weighed in my mind, and appointed Mr. Whatcoat and Mr. Vasey to go and serve the desolate sheep in America.[51]

The next day, 2 September 1784, Wesley recorded in his *Diary* that he had ordained Coke superintendant,[52] by the imposition of hands. Whatcoat's *Journal* mentions two ordinations for Whatcoat and Vasey, for deacon and elder respectively, on 1 and 2 September.[53] The Assistants ordained by John Wesley were admitted into the threefold order of deacon, elder and superintendant. But these were not Anglican orders, they were ordained as, and remained, Methodist Assistants. Wesley provided a certificate of ordination for Coke which stated:

To all to whom these Present shall come, John Wesley, late Fellow of Lincoln College in Oxford, Presbyter of the Church of England, sendeth greetings.

Whereas many of the People in the Southern Provinces of North America who desire to continue under my care, and still adhere to the Doctrines and Discipline of the Church of England are greatly distressed for want of Ministers to administer the Sacraments of Baptism and the Lord's Supper according to the usage of the same Church: And whereas there does not appear to be any other way of Supplying them with Ministers:

Know all men, that I John Wesley think myself to be providentially called at this time to set apart some persons for the work of ministry in America. And therefore under the Protection of almighty God, and with a single eye to his Glory, I have this day set apart as a Superintendent, by the imposition of my hands and prayer, (being assisted by other ordained Ministers) Thomas Coke, Doctor of Civil Law, a Presbyter of the Church of England, and a man whom I judge to be well qualified for that great work. And I do hereby recommend him to all whom it may concern as a fit person to preside over the Flock of Christ. In testimony whereof I have hereunto set my hand and seal this second day of September in the year of our Lord one thousand seven hundred and eighty four. John Wesley.[54]

John Wesley's letter to America, sent along with the newly ordained workers, further stated his understanding of the situation:

To our Brethren in North America.

1.   By a very uncommon train of Providences many of the Provinces of North America are totally disjoined from their Mother Country and erected into independent States. The English Government has no authority over them, either civil or

---

51   Curnock, *Journal*, 7:15.

52   'Superintendant' rather than 'Superintendent' was John Wesley's spelling of the word in his ordinal, *The Form and Manner of Making and Ordaining Superintendants, Elders, and Deacons* which he first published in *The Sunday Service of the Methodists in North America (1784)*. This work will follow Wesley's spelling in all cases except for those quotations where the original does not follow Wesley.

53   See *The Proceedings of the Wesley Historical Society* 7 (1911): 9.

54   Rupert Davies, A. Raymond George, and Gordon Rupp (eds), *A History of the Methodist Church in Great Britain*, 4 vols, (London: Epworth, 1965–88), 4:199–200.

ecclesiastical, any more than over the States of Holland. A civil authority is exercised over them, partly by the Congress, partly by the Provincial Assemblies. But no one either exercises or claims any ecclesiastical authority at all. In this particular situation some thousands of the inhabitants of these States desire my advice; and in compliance with their desire I have drawn up a little sketch.

2.   Lord King's *Account of the Primitive Church* convinced me many years ago that Bishops and presbyters are the same order, and consequently have the same right to ordain. For many years I have been importuned from time to time to exercise this right by ordaining part of our travelling preachers. But I have still refused, not only for peace' sake, but because I was determined as little as possible to violate the established order of the National Church to which I belonged.

3.   But the case is widely different between England and North America. Here there are Bishops who have a legal jurisdiction: in America there are none, neither any parish ministers. So that for some hundred miles together there is none either to baptize or to administer the Lord's Supper. Here, therefore, my scruples are at an end; and I conceive myself at full liberty, as I violate no order and invade no man's right by appointing and sending labourers into the harvest.

4.   I have accordingly appointed Dr. Coke and Mr. Francis Asbury to be Joint Superintendents over our brethren in North America; as also Richard Whatcoat and Thomas Vasey to act as elders among them, by baptizing and administering the Lord's Supper. And I have prepared a Liturgy little differing from that of the Church of England (I think the best constituted National Church in the World), which I advise all the travelling preachers to use on the Lord's Day in all the congregations, reading the Litany only on Wednesdays and Fridays and praying extempore on all other days. I also advise the elders to administer the Supper of the Lord on every Lord's Day.

5.   If any one will point out to me a more rational and scriptural; way of feeding and guiding those poor sheep in the wilderness, I will gladly embrace it. At present I cannot see any better method than that I have taken.

6.   It has, indeed, been proposed to desire the English Bishops to ordain part of our preachers for America. But to this I object; (1) I desired the Bishop of London to ordain only one, but could not prevail. (2) If they consented, we know the slowness of their proceedings; but the matter admits no delay. (3) If they would ordain them now, they would likewise expect to govern them. And how grievously would this entangle us! (4) As our American brethren are now totally disentangled both from the State and from the English hierarchy, we dare not entangle them again either with the none or the other. They are now at full liberty simply to follow the Scriptures and the Primitive Church. And we judge it best that they should stand fast in that liberty wherewith God has so strangely made them free.[55]

In his justification of having ordained Coke to the ministry of superintendant, John Wesley suggested that it was his reading of King's *Enquiry* which had led him to the conclusion that as a presbyter he could ordain. Later, Thomas Coke and

---

55   Telford, *Letters*, 7:237–9, 10 September 1784 'To our Brethren in North America'.

Francis Asbury would point to the precedent of the ancient church of Alexandria, which elected Bishops from among the presbytery, in justification of their taking up episcopal offices.

Nonetheless, exactly what John Wesley believed he was doing when he ordained men to the threefold order of deacon, elder and superintendant, may never be fully understood. Even though he had performed the ordination, Wesley remained adamant that he was loyal to the Church of England, for he acted in the capacity of the scriptural *episcopos* of the people called Methodists, ordaining Methodist preachers, not as Anglican presbyter ordaining men to Anglican orders. The fact remains that as an Anglican Priest he had no right whatsoever to ordain anybody to any office. John Wesley had so blinded himself by his interpretation of the authority which was his to exercise that he failed completely to comprehend the impact of his actions upon those around him.

In November 1784, Methodist preacher John Pawson, in a letter to John Atlay, teasingly asked:

> What do you think of the Revd. Mr. Vasey and the Revd. Dickey Whatcoat? 'Is Saul also among the prophets?' Must I write to the Revd. Mr. Atlay? Why not? Is not your right to that high and holy order as good in law as those who are transported? Well, well, who are the High Church Men now? The Priests of the high places, or the men of low degree, such as you and me. Will not Mr. Charles think that his brother has committed the sin of Jeroboam? For he really has made priests of the lowest Preachers however. This cannot be deny'd. All is well that ends well. I really care nothing at all about it, if it only answers good in the end. Neither do I care for any Church upon earth but the Church of the first-born whose names are written in Heaven. If this prospers, my soul rejoices, yea and shall rejoice, come what will.[56]

'Mr Charles,' that is Charles Wesley, was indeed unimpressed by the development. He commented:

> I can scarcely believe it, that, in his eighty-second year, my brother, my old intimate friend and companion, should have assumed the episcopal character, ordained elders, consecrated a Bishop, and sent him to ordain our lay preachers in America! ... Had they patience a little longer, they would have seen a real Bishop in America, consecrated by three Scotch Bishops who had their consecration from the English Bishops, and are acknowledged by them as the same with themselves ... But what are your poor Methodists now? Only a new sect of Presbyterians.[57]

Robert Monk has suggested that the similarities between Wesley's ordinations and those of the Presbyterians are clear. 'Ordination,' he wrote, 'is a corporate act joined in by more than one presbyter. It is the action of a presbytery signifying the unified body.'[58] Monk continued to suggest that Charles Wesley also recognised

56   John C. Bowmer and John A. Vickers (eds), *The Letters of John Pawson (Methodist itinerant, 1762–1806)*, (Peterborough: Methodist Publishing House 1994), 1:28.

57   Luke Tyerman, *The Life and Times of the Rev. John Wesley*, 3:439–40.

58   Robert C. Monk, *John Wesley: His Puritan Heritage*, (London: Epworth, 1966), 206.

the similarity between the Methodist ordinations and those of the Presbyterians. Charles Wesley apparently could see no future for Methodists, for they, through 'vain janglings' will 'like other sects of Dissenters, come to nothing.'[59]

Monk was wrong to suggest that the ordinations performed by John Wesley were presbyteral ordination. John Wesley intended them as episcopal ordinations, he was acting in his capacity as the scriptural *episcopos* of the people called Methodists. Furthermore, it can be asserted that it was Wesley's intention to establish the Methodist Church in America upon an episcopal system of government. If presbyteral ordination and polity were intended, then John Wesley would have had no need to ordain Thomas Coke as a Superintendant, for he was a presbyter in the Church of England already.

Charles Wesley was vehement in his opposition to the ordination of the Methodists. Nor was he only opposed to ordination for England, but was against such developments for America, Scotland and the Mission field. The force of his opposition, and the strength of his feeling, was given expression in a number of poems. Kimbrough and Beckerlegge have collected together many of the writings of Charles Wesley, amongst them a number relating to the ordinations performed by his brother. In these poems Charles Wesley accuses his brother of having forsaken good sense and turned into a schismatic.[60] He also turns he wrath upon Coke, writing:

A Roman emperor, 'tis said,
His favourite horse a consul made:
But Coke brings greater things to pass –
He makes a Bishop of an ass. [61]

At another time, he recalled, 'Happy the days, when Charles and John by nature and by grace were one ... and urg'd ... each other on'.[62] The poem continues to lament that it might have been better had John Wesley died before the day upon which he set out to ordain his preachers. Charles Wesley, rightly asks, 'W[esley] his hands on C[oke] hath laid, But who laid hands on him?' [63] The poet seems resigned to the situation when he writes:

---

59   Robert C. Monk, *John Wesley: His Puritan Heritage*, 207.

60   S.T. Kimbrough, Jr. and Oliver A. Beckerlegge (eds) *The Unpublished Poetry of Charles Wesley*, vol 3, *Hymns and Poems for Church and World* (Nashville: Kingswood, 1992), 81.

61   S.T. Kimbrough, Jr and Oliver A. Beckerlegge (eds), *The Unpublished Poetry of Charles Wesley*, 3:81.

62   S.T. Kimbrough, Jr and Oliver A. Beckerlegge (eds), *The Unpublished Poetry of Charles Wesley*, 3:82.

63   S.T. Kimbrough, Jr and Oliver A. Beckerlegge (eds), *The Unpublished Poetry of Charles Wesley*, 3:89.

'Tis done! the deed adventurous is done!
The sword is drawn, the civil war begun.
And John at last has pass'd the Rubicon! [64]

In a poem addressed directly to his brother, Charles reflects upon the manner in which John Wesley has explained and justified his actions.[65] Charles is clearly unimpressed by his brother's exposition, suggesting it is for self-gratification, rather than the alleviation of the American church's need, that motivates the ordinations.

You say, Th'Americans distrest
Unite your Consel to request:
I doubt, if they indeed require it,
Or you desire them to desire it:
I fear, your pure benevolence
And care of souls, is meer pretence
Your own desires to gratify,
That dying, you may never die,
But vindicate your sacred Claim,
And purchase an immortal Name.[66]

Charles continues his challenging reflection, casting doubts upon his brother's use of the writing of King and Stillingfleet as historic warrant for his action. He asks:

Wou'd King's weak reasons have prevail'd
Had not your Solid judgement fail'd,
Had not your wavering heart misled,
And got the better of your head? [67]

Charles continues his condemnation and turns his attention to John Wesley's adaptation of the Prayer Book, rightly observing and lamenting:

You tell us, with her Book of prayer
No book is worthy to compare?
Why change it then for your Edition,
Deprav'd by many a bold omission?

The Articles curtail'd must be,
To compliment Presbytery:
The Saints alas & Martyrs are

---

64   S.T. Kimbrough, Jr and Oliver A. Beckerlegge (eds), *The Unpublished Poetry of Charles Wesley*, 3:91.

65   S.T. Kimbrough, Jr and Oliver A. Beckerlegge (eds), *The Unpublished Poetry of Charles Wesley*, 3:95–101.

66   S.T. Kimbrough, Jr and Oliver A. Beckerlegge (eds), *The Unpublished Poetry of Charles Wesley*, 3:95–101.

67   S.T. Kimbrough, Jr and Oliver A. Beckerlegge (eds), *The Unpublished Poetry of Charles Wesley*, 3:95–101.

All purg'd out of your Calendar,
Since you for Saints acknowle[d]ge none
Except the Saints of Forty-One,
With their fanatical Descendants,
The noble House of Independents![68]

Again, Charles Wesley accredits his brother's action to pride and the desire to make a name for himself, asking, 'How is it possible to hide from your own heart its closest pride? Pride only gave the dire occasion of your clandestine Ordination.'[69]

The *Proceedings of the Wesley Historical Society* contains a set of articles, published over a span of fifty-three years, which tabulate the various acts of ordination undertaken by John Wesley and his early successors. The 1914 article by J.S. Simon combines with supplementary work published in 1943 by Frank Baker, in 1961 by Edward Lacey, and in 1967 by John Bowmer to form a significant contribution to work in this area.[70]

The purpose of the authors' task was outlined by Simon:

As our *Proceedings* do not, up to the present, contain a list of John Wesley's ordinations of his preachers we will make an attempt to provide materials for such a list.[71]

Simon prefaces his article with an overview of Wesley's practice of, and statements concerning, ordination of his preachers. His primary source is stated as being Curnock's edition of John Wesley's *Diary*, from which he compiles a list of Wesley's ordinations, beginning in 1784 with Whatcoat, Vasey and Coke. Simon's article differs from the later works in that he assesses each event, discussing its occasion, in the main body of text. The later articles are more properly lists, stating names of ordinands along with their intended destination, date and place of ordinations, and the source of further information.

Baker, Lacy and Bowmer build upon Simon's work. Baker explicitly cites Simon as source, but adds to it from sources available to the later writer.[72] Lacy observes that since Baker's article a few more facts have come to light. He states that his work is dependent upon Baker's work, but also seeks to incorporate all the

---

68   S.T. Kimbrough, Jr. and Oliver A. Beckerlegge (eds) *The Unpublished Poetry of Charles Wesley*, 3:95–101.

69   S.T. Kimbrough, Jr. and Oliver A. Beckerlegge (eds) *The Unpublished Poetry of Charles Wesley*, 3:95–101.

70   J.S.Simon, *Wesley's Ordinations*, in *The Proceedings of the Wesley Historical Society*, 9 (1913-14):145–54; Frank Baker, *Wesley's Ordinations*, in *The Proceedings of the Wesley Historical Society*, 24 (1943):76; H. Edward Lacey, John *Wesley's Ordinations*, in *The Proceedings of the Wesley Historical Society*, 33 (1961):118; John C. Bowmer, *Ordinations in Methodism 1791-1836*, in *The Proceedings of the Wesley Historical Society*, 36 (1967–8):121–7.

71   *The Proceedings of the Wesley Historical Society*, 9 (1913–4):145.

72   *The Proceedings of the Wesley Historical Society*, 24 (1943):76.

recent findings.[73] Bowmer's work of 1967 seeks to extend the work of Simon, Baker and Lacy, to cover the period after Wesley's death to 1835, when general ordination by prayer and the imposition of hands were reintroduced into the Wesleyan polity.

Lacy has suggested that the sources of information are not completely reliable:

> Wesley did not always record his ordinations, as for instance that of Atmore. There may therefore have been others which may one day come to light.[74]

On 1 August 1785 John Wesley ordained three Methodists for Scotland on the same basis as for America. One of these was John Pawson, who, anticipating the event in a letter to Charles Atmore, wrote:

> Strange to think of it, I am going to Edinburgh! But more strange still, I am going to be ordained by Mr. Wesley and Dr. Coke next Monday morning at 5 o'clock. Wonders, you may well say, never cease.[75]

Many of the episcopalian clergymen in Scotland refused to admit Methodists to the sacraments, except on condition that they renounce their associations with Wesley. The established presbyterian Church of Scotland was more benevolent to the Methodists, but Wesley was not happy to leave this as the solution. Writing on 1 August 1785, John Wesley stated:

> Having with a few select friends weighed the matter thoroughly, I yielded to their judgement, and set apart three of our well-tried preachers, John Pawson, Thomas Hanby and Joseph Taylor, to minister in Scotland; and I trust God will bless their ministrations, and show that he has sent them.[76]

It is important to notice that none of these ordinations were of Methodist preachers to work in England. Although John Wesley was being pressed by the English Methodists to ordain preachers for the work, he had not done so because the Church of England was the established national church. For Wesley to ordain for England would, he understood, be to step beyond the fellowship of that Church; a move which he still considered both illegal and inexpedient. There being no established national church in America meant that he was free to ordain his Assistants and so to initiate a new church. Presumably, Wesley felt that he could ordain for Scotland because the established church there was Presbyterian and not Episcopalian. Dennis Campbell has written:

> The problem in England then, was not theological but legal. Theologically Wesley judged that he was acting as a Bishop to the Methodists both in England and in America. In England legal provisions of the established church caused him to refrain from using

73   The *Proceedings* of the Wesley Historical Society, 33 (1961):118.
74   The *Proceedings* of the Wesley Historical Society, 33 (1961):118.
75   John C. Bowmer and John A. Vickers (eds), *The Letters of John Pawson (Methodist itinerant, 1762–1806)*, (Peterborough: Methodist Publishing House, 1994), 1:29.
76   Curnock, *Journal*, 7:101.

the prerogative of a Bishop to ordain, but no such limitation applied in the case of America.[77]

On 18 August 1785, John Wesley wrote to his brother Charles:

For these forty years I have been in doubt concerning that question, 'What obedience is due to "Heathenish priests and mitred infidels"?' I have from time to time proposed my doubts to the most pious and sensible clergymen I knew. But they gave me no satisfaction; rather they seemed to be puzzled as well as me.

Some obedience I always paid to the Bishops in obedience to the laws of the land. But I cannot see that I am under any obligation to obey them further than those laws require.

It is in obedience to those laws that I have never exercised in England the power which I believe God has given me. I firmly believe I am a scriptural episcopos as much as any man in England or in Europe; for the uninterrupted succession I know to be a fable, which no man ever did or can prove. But this does in no wise interfere with my remaining in the Church of England; from which I have no more desire to separate than I had fifty years ago.[78]

On 28 and 29 July 1786, at Bristol, John Wesley ordained Warrener, Hammett, and Clarke for work on the mission field and Keighley and Charles Atmore for work in Scotland. Ordinations for England were precipitated by the issue of the societies not being able to meet the sacramental needs of the people, many having been rejected from the parish church. Taylor and Hanby, ordained for Scotland, assumed the ministerial function in England.

In August 1787 John Pawson wrote to Charles Atmore, recounting the Methodist Conference which had just finished:

Mr. W[esley] seems more determined to abide in the Church than ever. He talked about it, and about it again in the public Conference, in the Society, etc., and in such a hot, fiery spirit as I did not like to see. He talked of fighting with a flail, etc., and of putting all out of the Society who do not go to the Church. We are to be just as, and what we were, in every respect before we came to Scotland. No Sacraments, no gowns, no nothing at all, of any kind or sort whatsoever ... Charles Wesley, the Sunday before the Conference spoke in the Society in London to this effect – 'I told you 40 years ago that from among yourselves grievous wolves would arise who would rend and tear the flock. You now see my words fulfilled. These self-created Bishops and self-made Priests are the very men; but I charge you all in the presence of God never receive the Sacrament of any of them, etc ...' So you see that he has fairly discharged the people from receiving the Sacrament of his own brother; for who but he is the self-created Bishop? O cursed prejudice! O furious bigotry! How does the fire from hell burn in that poor miserable man's breast ... Solomon says there is no new thing under the sun; but here we see something which I believe was never known in the Christian Church before – that men approved of God and their brethren, and that for many years, should be regularly ordained and act in the capacity of ministers, and that with full approbation and success,

---

77   Dennis M. Campbell, *The Yoke of Obedience: The Meaning of Ordination in Methodism,* (Nashville: Abingdon, 1988), 63.

78   Telford, *Letters,* 7:284–5. To Charles Wesley 19 August 1785.

should be deposed from that office by one single man, and that without any crime committed, great or small, real or pretended. Do you think now that even the Pope himself ever acted such a part as this? No, never! What an astonishing degree of power does our aged Father and Friend exercise. What do you think that the Scotch ministers would say, did they know of this? However, I am satisfied, and have nothing but love in my heart towards the good old man. But really, it will not bear the light at all.[79]

In October 1787 John Pawson, who had been ordained for the work in Scotland, wrote from Leeds to Charles Atmore at Glasgow:

The people at Hunslet, near Leeds are very desirous of having the Sacrament. I wrote to Mr. Wesley about it, and [he] desires me to do nothing in that way until I have read a sermon he is going to publish in order to prove that wicked ministers may do good to their congregations.[80] I have promised him I will not, and something to this effect: I value the Methodist Connection beyond all ordinations upon earth. As to your intended sermon, I think you will find it difficult to prove that point, because our Lord says, 'Do men gather grapes of thorns or figs of thistles?', and because it is also said, 'I have not sent them, therefore they shall not profit this people at all.' There are indeed some things which appear strange to me. You did indeed ordain us, and you said, 'Take thou authority to preach God's holy Word and to administer his holy Sacraments.' I have done so, and now you have suspended us without charging us with any crime. This I think is a new thing in the world: a thing never heard of in the Christian Church before. Ordination by Presbyters was never disallowed by the Church of England till the time of Bishop Bancroft,[81] and was never made unlawful till the Act of Uniformity[82] made it so; and I think that every good man will acknowledge that that said Act was the greatest curse to the Church of England that ever befell it. But now it seems to me that we are drinking into [*sic*] the spirit of Bancroft and those who made that Act, if you say No. We persecute no man. What is the reason you do not? Why we humbly submit; else would you not turn us out of the Connection? And what is this but persecution?' All the answers he returned was, A new thing in the world! That a priest should forbear to exercise his office; I myself have done this for 40 years in Scotland, etc. Pray who would receive it at his hand on Scotland in his way? and in the room of our being suspended. He says forbear, as if we did this by our own choice, as he has done. O what quibbling is this! Supposing any was to order Mr. W. to forbear exercising his Priestly Office, would he forbear also? I trow not! All this little affects me, only I wish to see sincerity, truth, integrity and consistency in this great man, to write to me in Scotland, Revd., as if he had made me something I was not before and now in England just the contrary. I told him that he now seemed to pour contempt upon his own work. But he must have his own way.[83]

79   John C. Bowmer and John A. Vickers (eds), *The Letters of John Pawson*, 1: 46.

80   Wesley's sermon 'On Attending the Church Service' was published the following year both in *Sermons on Several Occasions* vol. 8, and in the *Arminian Magazine*.

81   Richard Bancroft (1544–1610), Archbishop of Canterbury and opponent of Puritanism and Presbyterianism.

82   The editors of Pawson's letter identify that it is the 1662 version of the Act which is being referred to here.

83   John C. Bowmer and John A. Vickers (eds), *The Letters of John Pawson*, 1: 51.

Matters were made worse when some of the preachers began to take the office upon themselves without Wesley's authorisation. Pawson, again, in a letter to Charles Atmore dated 16 September 1788, tells:

> Mr. Hanby writes that he intended to preach in his gown next Sunday and he talks of administering the Sacrament at Nottingham very shortly. I am very glad to hear it and shall not be in the least sorry to hear the same thing of you: but I think that you should use the Prayer Book or the good old man will not be well pleased with you. The people will like it much better than they think when they hear it read in a lively manner. I have begun to read it at Hunslet and the people in general as far as I hear are much satisfied. I think that it may be introduced in Leeds in a little while. I have had two conversations with the Leaders about it and I had a great majority on my side; but we have 4 or 5 who are sufficiently bigotted [sic] in all reason. If I only know Mr. Wesley's mind, I should then know how to act.[84]

A further letter from Pawson to Atmore, dated 11 December 1788, tells of the reaction to the administering of the sacraments at Newark and Nottingham:

> Mr. Hanby writes that they have given the Sacrament publicly at Newark and privately at Nottingham at the earnest request of the people in general; but Mr. Mather got to hear of it and wrote Joseph Taylor such a thundering letter about it that Joseph was quite frightened and before he had seen Mr. Hanby wrote a very humble and submissive letter to Mr. Wesley who wrote for answer, that we are resolved to abide in the Church and therefore desired that they would do it no more ... When shall we be free from those chains of our old Egyptian Mother, think you?[85]

In January 1789, Pawson again to Atmore, reported that:

> Mr. Hanby writes ... and is fully determined to continue administering the Sacrament, let the consequence be what it will. He says that he is so clearly satisfied [of] the approbation of God that he feels his mind quite w[illing] to suffer anything rather than give it up. I am exceeding glad to hear he has so much Christian courage, and I hope that the Lord will support, and bring him safely through. Poor Joseph Taylor has quite given it up.[86]

Pawson began to reveal his hand more clearly, writing again to Atmore, in March 1789:

> Mr. Hanby ... goes on administering the Sacrament and seems determined to do it at all events ... Mr. Mather wants me to write to Mr. Hanby and to desire him to give it up. This I dare not do, because I really think he is acting right... I expect that if Mr. Wesley lives till the Conference, Mr. Hanby will be greatly opposed, as no doubt many will have something to say against him as to his present proceedings, were it only to please Mr. Wesley as they may suppose. If the Preachers could only be quiet, I make no doubt but Mr. Wesley would at least connive at what has been done.[87]

---

84 John C. Bowmer and John A. Vickers (eds), *The Letters of John Pawson*, 1: 68.
85 John C. Bowmer and John A. Vickers (eds), *The Letters of John Pawson*, 1: 74.
86 John C. Bowmer and John A. Vickers (eds), *The Letters of John Pawson*, 1: 76.
87 John C. Bowmer and John A. Vickers (eds), *The Letters of John Pawson*, 1: 78.

Feelings were running high as ordinations were available everywhere except England. John Wesley's resistance was beginning to wane. With the death of Charles Wesley in 1788, the main source of opposition was removed. English ordinations took place; on 6 and 7 August 1788 Alexander Mather was ordained, and on 25 and 27 February 1789 Thomas Rankin and Henry Moore received ordination into the two orders of deacon and elder.

Henry Moore's ordination certificate, dated 27 February 1789, is a document of great importance.[88] The certificate declared that, in the opinion of John Wesley, Moore was a man qualified to feed the flock of Christ, and to administer the sacraments of baptism and the Lord's Supper, *according to the usage of the Church of England.*[89]

John Pawson, in a letter published by Tyerman in his *Life and Times of the Revd. John Wesley*, makes suggestions as to Wesley's intentions:

> Mr. Wesley knew that the state of societies in England required such measures to be taken, or many of the people would leave the Connexion ... He foresaw that the Methodists would soon become a distinct body. He was deeply prejudiced against presbyterian, and was much in favour of episcopal government. In order, therefore, to preserve all that is valuable in the Church of England among the Methodists, he ordained Mr. Mather and Dr. Coke, Bishops. These he undoubtedly designed should ordain others.[90]

When Wesley did undertake the ordinations of his preachers it was, in his mind, for specific and essential purposes. As ever, he was motivated by the demands which his evangelistic calling placed upon him. When faced with the problem of what he regarded as spiritual deprivation of men and women dying in ignorance and being damned, Wesley believed that he dare not delay a moment longer. He believed that the demands of the Gospel required him to ordain his preachers, first for America, then for Scotland and, ultimately, for work in England. It is, though, important to remember that Wesley intended that he ordain his associates as Methodist preachers, not to Anglican orders.

Furthermore, these ordinations were not intended to signal the general elevation to a sacramental ministry of those who had previously been appointed only as preachers. Wesley expected his people to remain in the work for which they had been called and to which he had appointed them.

---

88   Facsimile to be found in the Curnock edition of Wesley's *Journal*, 8: 505.
89   Present writer's italics.
90   Luke Tyerman, *Life and Times of John Wesley*, 3:443.

Chapter 6

Wesley Reflects upon his Actions
'Prophets and Priests' – Ireland 1789

On Sunday 12 July 1789, less than two years before his death, John Wesley completed what was to be his last visit to the Methodist people in Ireland.[1] The visit, which had begun the previous March, had proved to be a great trial for the octogenarian Churchman. The Irish Methodists were feeling increasingly put out by John Wesley's insistence that they, like the English Methodists, should remain faithful to the Church of England. The people wanted the Methodist societies to be separated from the Church, and their preachers to be allowed to administer the sacraments.

John Wesley insisted that ordination by prayer and the imposition of hands was the only right means of appointing his preachers to a sacramental ministry. In September 1784 he had ordained Methodists for such work in America, later making similar provision for the ministry in Scotland,[2] the Mission Field,[3] and England.[4] Just one month before his arrival in Ireland, John Wesley had ordained Thomas Rankin and Henry Moore for work in England.[5] Seeing Wesley's practice elsewhere caused the Irish Methodists to add further vigour to the already forceful expression of their cause. Put simply, they wanted what everybody else seemed to be getting.

Soon after arriving in Ireland, John Wesley assessed the situation and found it showed a great improvement upon his experience in the country two years earlier.[6] During his previous visit, Wesley had discovered that many of the Irish Methodists had turned away from attendance at the Parish Churches, preferring instead to attend either the dissenting meeting house or only the Methodist meetings. The practice had led to an increased feeling, amongst the members of the Irish societies, that they should separate themselves from the Church. John Wesley reached a compromise. The society members agreed to attend the Parish Church on the first Sunday of the month. He allowed that, on other Sundays, they would meet

---

1   For a full account, see Curnock, *Journal*, 7:481–519.

2   1 August 1785 and July 1786.

3   28/29 July 1786.

4   6/7 August 1788 and February 1789.

5   See Curnock, *Journal*, 7:471.

6   For an account of the earlier visit to Ireland (April–July 1787) see Curnock, *Journal*, 7:258f, and for his assessment of that visit compared with his later visit, see the same volume p482f.

in their own rooms to use the Church Service, that is the office of Morning Prayer, presumably in the form published in *The Sunday Service*.[7] Writing in his *Journal* for Monday 30 March 1789, John Wesley bore testimony to the success of this scheme. He identified the purpose as having been to prevent the separation from the Church of England:

> The effect was (1) that they went more to the meetings; (2) that three times more went to St. Patrick's (perhaps six times) in six or twelve months than had done for ten or twenty years before. Observe! This is done not to prepare for, but to prevent, a separation from the Church.[8]

Whilst in Ireland, John Wesley seemed often to find himself having to explain his expectations of, and intentions for, the Methodist societies. On Easter Day, 12 April 1789, he met with the society in Dublin and explained that the original design of the Methodists was not to be a distinct party, '… but to stir up all parties … to worship God in spirit and in truth.'[9] Wesley reiterated this point of view the following day, when he visited the Methodists at Tyrrell's Pass.[10] Albert Outler has suggested the issue of separation was the cause of the dispute that, on 17 April 1789, Wesley found raging between the members and his Assistant at Athlone.[11] Again, at Cork, on 10 May 1789, John Wesley spoke with the members of the society, undoubtedly on the subject of separation.[12] He recorded in his *Journal*:

> I was enabled to speak with power in the evening to more than the house could contain, and afterwards to the society. May God write it on all their hearts! I am now clear of their blood.[13]

John Wesley's efforts at convincing the Irish Methodists of the necessity of staying faithful to the Church of England seem to have met with some success, at least as far as the preachers who met him in Conference were concerned. The entry in his *Journal* for 3 July 1789 recorded that he found the Methodists united in their decision not to leave the Church.[14] Wesley added the encouraging comment that 'It is no wonder that there has been this year so large an increase of the society.'[15]

---

7   John Wesley's Abridgement of the *Book of Common Prayer (1662)* which had been published in 1784 for the use of the Methodists in North America. The *Sunday Service* was subsequently republished in a number of versions for the use of the Methodists elsewhere.

8   Curnock, *Journal, 7*:482.

9   Curnock, *Journal, 7*:486.

10   Curnock, *Journal, 7*:487.

11   See Outler's 'Introductory Comment' to *Sermon 121 Prophets and Priests* in *Works*, 4:72.

12   Wesley had completed his Sermon, dealt with in this work as *Prophets and Priests*, on 9 May 1798. Thus the assertion that the content of that sermon would have been foremost in his mind when meeting with the Methodists on the following day.

13   Curnock, *Journal, 7*:494.

14   Curnock, *Journal, 7*:516.

15   Curnock, *Journal, 7*:516.

Later in the Conference, Wesley declared that he believed the Irish preachers had 'sound experience, deep piety and strong understanding.'[16]

John Wesley was anxious that people should understand his opinions about his preachers taking up a sacramental ministry and separation from the Church. Whilst in Ireland he had, at every opportunity, addressed the topics in his conversations with the societies. After the visit, Wesley put his thoughts into print in the *Arminian Magazine*.[17] In May and June 1790, the magazine carried the sermon that he had completed whilst at Cork the previous year, addressing questions of ministry, ordination and separation.[18] Originally this sermon, which Outler has suggested is more like an essay,[19] was untitled and known simply as *Sermon 57*. Wesley's reference to the priestly families of the Old Testament led to the work becoming known as the *Korah Sermon*. The nineteenth-century editor of Wesley's *Works*, Thomas Jackson, re-labelled it *On the Ministerial Office*.[20] More recently, Albert Outler has given it the title *Prophets and Priests*.[21]

Although there is no evidence of *Prophets and Priests* having ever been preached, the ideas expressed in it are in line with those put forward by Wesley in Ireland and elsewhere.[22] The sermon presented a résumé of John Wesley's use of his preachers, in particular revealing the way in which they were subject to his authority. The kernel of the sermon was that the Methodist preachers were appointed, by John Wesley, to the work of preaching; they were not to take other work upon themselves, certainly not the administration of the sacraments, without further appointment by him.

John Wesley took the text for his sermon from Hebrews 5:4, 'No man taketh this honour unto himself, but he that is called of God, as was Aaron.' He began with a defence of his preachers conscious of the criticisms that were being levelled against them. It was accepted that God's call of a person to be a preacher must be tested by the Church. The inward call from God was reckoned as insufficient without the outward call from the Church, 'as Aaron "was called of God" by Moses.'[23] It was widely believed that the only proper test of such a sense of call was to submit oneself to examination for holy orders. The belief that ordination was a prerequisite for preaching naturally led to the conclusion that lay people

---

16   Curnock, *Journal*, 7:517.

17   April, May and June 1790. The April publication concerned separation from the Church whilst those of May and June were the sermon here referred to as *Prophets and Priests*.

18   Wesley had completed this sermon on 9 May 1789.

19   Albert C. Outler (ed.), *Works*, 4:72.

20   Jackson, *Works*, 7.

21   Albert C. Outler (ed.), *Works*, 4:75. For the sake of convenience, this work will follow Outler's designation of the sermon as *Prophets and Priests*.

22   As early as 1755, John Wesley was expressing the opinion that he had no intention of separating from the established Church of England. See, for example, his letter to Samuel Walker, 24 September 1755, in Baker, *Letters*, 2:592–6 and Telford, *Letters*, 3:146.

23   Albert C. Outler (ed.), *Works*, 4:75.

should not preach.[24] Wesley countered the suggestion with the observation that Aaron was not called to be a preacher, but a priest; whereas his Assistants and preachers were not called to be priests, but preachers.

The purpose of Wesley's sermon was not apologetic but didactic. He was not intending to give a defence of the use of his workers for some outside group, but to show those associated with him how he expected them to respond to his authority. Therefore, he used the text to call back into line the preachers who were moving towards taking a sacramental ministry upon themselves. Such a ministry, suggested Wesley, must depend upon the call of God confirmed by the call of the Church. The call felt by the preachers must depend, for confirmation, upon appointment by John Wesley. In this context, the Methodists were Aaron and Wesley their Moses!

Despite his having already ordained a number of his associates, Wesley forbad others taking such work upon themselves, suggesting that it would lead to separation from the Church. The implication of Wesley's action was that the ordinations he had performed had been for situations in which he felt there to be no threat to the relationship of the Methodists and the Church. The indiscriminate adoption of a sacramental ministry by his preachers could only lead to schism. Therefore, unless he appointed them otherwise, the Methodists were to be preachers only.

Wesley emphasised his intention for those in connection with him only being preachers by telling the story of their origins. He wrote of Maxfield, Richards, and Westell being received as his Assistants:

> Let it be well observed on what terms we received these, viz., as prophets, not as priests. We receive them wholly and solely to preach, not to administer the sacraments. And those who imagine these offices to be inseparably joined are totally ignorant of the constitution of the whole Jewish as well as Christian Church ... Otherwise we should never have accepted the service, either of Mr. Maxfield, Richards, or Westell.[25]

Wesley called to mind the Methodist Conference of 1744, at which the Assistants asked how they should consider themselves. They were told to regard themselves 'As extraordinary messengers, raised up to provoke the ordinary ones to jealousy.'[26] Mr. Wesley's Assistants were to be prophets, not priests.

It is important to recognise the context of *Prophets and Priests*. It was the statement, by Wesley for his society members, of his judgement concerning the issues of separation from the Church and the authorisation of his preachers to administer the sacraments. It was not an apologia concerning his use of Assistants, nor was the work intended for study beyond the Methodist societies. The sermon was a demonstration of John Wesley, the scriptural *episcopos* of the Methodist

---

24   This was a position commonly held amongst members of the Church of England during the period. In an editorial footnote to the sermon, Albert Outler has suggested the sermons of three clergymen in particular, Thomas Bisse (1708), William Roberts (1709) and Edward Cobden (1753). Albert C. Outler (ed.), *Works*, 4:75.

25   Albert C. Outler (ed.), *Works*, 4:78.

26   Albert C. Outler (ed.), *Works*, 4:78.

people, revealing his will and exerting his authority. It is the assessment of this authority, and of Wesley's expression of it, that is crucial to an understanding of his policy and practice concerning the ministry and ordination of his preachers.

The sermon embodied a discussion concerning original intentions, rather than the developed practice that had arisen from the particular situations in which Wesley had found himself. That Wesley had already ordained several of his preachers for a sacramental ministry was incidental to his line of argument. Wesley is seen arguing from his own viewpoint as founder of the movement. The founder of the movement choosing to vary his practice is one thing, for the members to do so is contrary to discipline. The discussion can be seen to revolve around Wesley's understanding and exercise of authority. Ultimately, one has to acknowledge that whatever Wesley chose to do, he could do, because he said he could!

The sermon reached its climax with Wesley declaring his love of the Church of England and rejecting all suggestion of his intending separation, even when he was at variance with it. To the observer, Wesley appeared, by his actions, to have separated himself from the Church. He, however, believed otherwise:

> I hold all the doctrines of the Church of England. I love her liturgy. I approve her plan of discipline, and only wish it could be put in execution. I do not knowingly vary from any rule of the Church, unless in those few instances, where I judge, and as far as I judge, there is absolute necessity.
>
> For instance,
>
> (1) As few clergymen open their Churches to me, I am under the necessity of preaching abroad.
>
> (2) As I know no forms that will suit all occasions, I am often under necessity of praying extempore.
>
> (3) In order to build up the flock of Christ in faith and love, I am under a necessity of uniting them together, and of dividing them into little companies, that they may provoke one another to love and good works.
>
> (4) That my fellow-labourers and I may more effectually assist each other, to save our own souls and those that hear us, I judge it necessary to meet the preachers, or at least a greater part of them, once a year.
>
> (5) In those conferences we fix the stations of all the preachers for the ensuing year.
>
> But all this is not separating from the Church. So far from it, that, whenever I have opportunity, I attend the Church service myself, and advise all our societies so to do.[27]

John Wesley declared that he would not separate from the Church of England, but, in cases of necessity, would vary from it. He called the Methodists to remain loyal to the Church, remaining in the place to which they had been appointed, continuing the work to which they had been called. Wesley called his preachers to

---

27   Albert C. Outler (ed.), *Works*, 4:81.

resist the temptation to take up any further work, other than that authorised by himself, lest it takes them outside the fellowship of the Church of England:

> I earnestly advise you, abide in your place; keep your own station. Ye were, fifty years ago, those of you that were then Methodist preachers, extraordinary messengers of God, not going in your own will, but thrust out, not to supersede, but to 'provoke to jealousy', the ordinary messengers. In God's name, stop there! Both by your preaching and example provoke them to love and to good works – a body of people who, being of no sect or party, are friends to all parties, and endeavour to forward all in heart-religion, in the knowledge and love of God and man. Ye yourselves were at first called in the Church of England; and though ye have and will have a thousand temptations to leave it, and set up for yourselves, regard them not; be Church of England men still; do not cast away the peculiar glory which God hath put upon you, and frustrate the design of providence, the very end for which God raised you up.[28]

The calling of God was, for John Wesley, the ultimate authority by which he tested both his own actions and those of his preachers. If the call he heard put him in conflict with the practices of the Church of his birth and ordination, then that Church must yield. Frequently John Wesley was taken by surprise at the direction in which that call took him. It was this sense of God's bidding which culminated in his accepting the use of lay people as preachers, as has been shown in the account of the appointment of Thomas Maxfield.[29] It is clear that despite the autocratic nature of John Wesley's rule of the Methodist people, he was willing to recognise that God's call to him might come through his people. John Wesley believed that all such occasions of call were to be tested. The ultimate test was that the work should bear fruit.

The image left by John Wesley, on the mind, is of a man driven by a vision. He was single-minded in the pursuit of the demands of that vision. He heard the call of God leading him into unknown places and constantly did strive to rationalise and explain the journey he was making, as well as to understand the places in which he found himself. In so seeking to rationalise, explain and understand, he hoped to share the vision, to communicate the demands of the call he had heard, with the Church of his day. For remember, John Wesley claimed never to intend to separate from the Church of England; his aim was its restoration as the means of salvation and the expression of the glory of God. The Methodist societies, working within the established Church, were intended as a means to realise this aim.

Throughout his life John Wesley maintained his iron-like grip upon the reins of Methodism. There was no adequate lieutenant to whom he would pass authority. He met in Conference with his preachers, but that Conference was not, yet, a legislative body apart from his direction. He was the scriptural *episcopos* of the people called Methodists, under God, the ultimate source of authority and approval for all they sought to do. There was remarkably little room for negotiation. This is how it was; if the people did not like it then they were free to leave his connexion.

---

28   Albert C. Outler (ed.), *Works*, 4:82.
29   See above, page 23.

Chapter 7

The Liturgy
Prayer Book Ordinal Adapted

When, in September 1784, John Wesley ordained Coke, Vasey and Whatcoat, he presumably used *The Form and Manner of Making and Ordaining of Superintendants, Elders and Deacons*, which formed part of his abridgement of the *Book of Common Prayer (1662)*. *The Form and Manner ...* was included among the *Occasional Services* of *The Sunday Service of the Methodists in North America*, (London, 1784), which Wesley sent to the colony along with the newly ordained men.

Although John Wesley published a number of editions of *The Sunday Service* for intended use in different locations, the text of the Ordinal remained constant.[1] The following commentary upon the first edition of the rite can, therefore, be taken as overall commentary on Wesley's revision of the Ordinal from the *Book of Common Prayer (1662)*.

In his revision of the Prayer Book Ordinal, John Wesley was meeting the specific needs of a church in a new situation. Although not believing there to be another liturgy of such 'solid, scriptural, rational piety, than the Common Prayer of the Church of England,'[2] Wesley realised that some modifications were needed before it would be acceptable in the newly independent country.

Many of John Wesley's modifications found their origins in the suggestions made by the Puritans at the Savoy Conference in May 1661.[3] The founder of Methodism had been introduced to the influences of Puritanism by his family, both of his grandfathers having suffered ejection from their livings on St Bartholomew's

---

1   The variety of these has been reviewed by Wesley F. Swift in his article *The Sunday Service of the Methodists* in The *Proceedings* of the Wesley Historical Society, 29 (1952–3). That the text of the Ordinal remains constant has been asserted by the present author using copies of the Sunday Service held in the British Methodist Archives at the John Rylands University Library of Manchester, Deansgate, Manchester, M3 3EH, UK.

2   John Wesley, *The Sunday Service of the Methodists in North America*, (London: William Strahan, 1784), Preface, Facsimile edition with notes by James F. White, *John Wesley's Prayer Book: The Sunday Service of the Methodists in North America*, (Cleveland: Order of Saint Luke, 1991).

3   A clear account of the Savoy Conference and the development of the *Book of Common Prayer (1662)*, along with a review of the various Puritan, Laudian and Nonjurors' suggestions for revision in the seventeenth and eighteenth centuries, can be found in R.C.D. Jasper, *The Development of the Anglican Liturgy 1662–1980*, (London: SPCK, 1989), 1–39.

Day, 24 August 1662.[4] It is known that in 1754 John Wesley had read, and been impressed by, Edmund Calamy's *Abridgement of Mr. Baxter's History of his life and Times.*[5] Indeed, it has been suggested that Wesley undertook his revision with Calamy's book in mind, if not in hand.[6] Furthermore, his revision of the *Book of Common Prayer (1662)* revealed many similarities with the proposals of John Jones and Theophilus Lindsey.[7]

Heitzenrater has suggested that John Wesley had wanted to improve the *Book of Common Prayer (1662)* ever since his association with Thomas Deacon and the Manchester nonjurors during his Oxford days, 'when they were trying to pattern liturgy and worship after the Early Church.'[8] At the Methodist Conference of 1755, Wesley had declared some of his objections to the *Book of Common Prayer (1662).*[9] In relation to the Ordinal, he objected to anything which suggested differences between bishops and priests. He also objected to the idea of priests forgiving sins, especially disliking the formula at the ordination of priests which stated that 'whatever sins ye remit, they are remitted.'[10]

James White has suggested that if Wesley's work had been available a century and a quarter earlier then it may have 'been acceptable to many desiring a

---

4   Under the provision of the Act of Uniformity of 1662, passed by the House of Commons in July 1661, all ministers were, by St Bartholomew's Day (24 August) 1661, to publicly accept without question 'all and everything contained and prescribed' in the *Book of Common Prayer (1662),* it becoming the standard of belief and practice. Those refusing to do so were removed from their livings.

5   Edmund Calamy (1671–1732) was a Protestant historian whose work threw great light upon the movements of nonconformity within the Church of England. A.E. Peaston, *The Prayer Book Tradition in the Free Churches,* (London: James Clarke & Co., 1964), 52.

6   Frederick. Hunter, *Sources of Wesley's Revision of the Prayer Book 1784-8,* Proceedings of the Wesley Historical Society, 23(1941–2):123–33.

7   John Jones, Vicar of Alconbury, in 1749 published *Free and Candid Disquisitions Relating to the Church of England and the Means of Advancing Religion Therein.* He wanted to encourage the reformation of the liturgy as a means of enabling the returning of Dissenters into the Church of England. He was particularly anxious to removed everything from the Prayer Book which could not be justified by appeal to Scripture. Theophilius Lindsey had become disenchanted with the Church of England and so left to form the Reformed Church of England. In 1774 he published *The Book of Common Prayer Reformed According to the Plan of the Late Dr. Samuel Clarke,* and followed it with an enlarged edition the following year. Despite the title of the work, there was little evidence of Lindsey's work owing very much to Samuel Clarke, it was mostly Lindsey's own work.

8   Richard P. Heitzenrater, *Wesley and the People Called Methodists,* 288–9

9   Frank Baker, *John Wesley and the Church of England,* 331.

10   A comprehensive discussion of Wesley's objections to the *Book of Common Prayer (1662),* relating to the other rites not under discussion in this work, can be found in James F. White, *John Wesley's Prayer Book: The Sunday Service of the Methodists in North America,* 7–14.

comprehensive national church.'[11] But, surely, if John Wesley had been around in the 1660s, he would almost certainly have suffered the same fate of expulsion from the established church as those whose ideas he followed. Indeed, in a letter of 1775, Wesley admits this himself:

> Those ministers who truly feared God near a hundred years ago had undoubtedly much the same objections to the Liturgy which some (who have never read their Works) have now. And I myself so far allow the force of several of those objections that I should not dare to declare my assent and consent to that book in the terms prescribed.[12]

English Anglican liturgical scholar R.C.D. Jasper has commented that 'what is surprising that Wesley produced such a book at all, in view of the large number of Puritans in America.'[13] Jasper also recalled the words of Rattenbury that 'A Dissenter in Wesley's time would have destroyed the Prayer Book, not revised it.'[14]

Despite the background to John Wesley's revisions of the Prayer Book, his work was conservative; he changed only what he considered necessary. His alterations were mostly matters of omission and abbreviation. Describing his work, Wesley said that 'I took particular care throughout to alter nothing for altering sake. In religion I am for as few innovations as possible. I love the old wine best.'[15]

John Wesley's revision of the Ordinal is visible from the beginning of the rite. He shortened the title of the Ordinal, removing the phrases 'and Consecrating' and 'According to the Order of the Church of England.' The oaths of allegiance to the King and Archbishops had no place in Wesley's revision. Indeed, all references to the English church, realm, and canon law, were removed. This was appropriate for the new church in America, for it was no longer under the civil rule of the English establishment.

All references to clerical vestments were taken from the rubrics. Wesley was producing an Ordinal for a frontier church with an itinerant ministry; not for an established church with buildings and settled ministry. The vestments of the Church of England, even if they had been available, were inappropriate forms of dress for the travelling preacher who would pass from settlement to settlement on horseback!

The nature of the infant church also made it necessary for John Wesley to remove all references to the singing of liturgical portions. It was one thing for his people to be encouraged to sing the hymns, which were set to popular tunes; it was

---

11   John Wesley, *The Sunday Service of the Methodists in North America*, (London: William Strahan, 1784), Preface, Facsimile edition with notes by James F. White, *John Wesley's Prayer Book: The Sunday Service of the Methodists in North America*, 7.

12   Telford, *Letters*, 3:152. To Samuel Walker, 20 November 1755.

13   R.C.D. Jasper, *The Development of the Anglican Liturgy 1662–1980*, 19.

14   R.C.D. Jasper, *The Development of the Anglican Liturgy 1662–1980*, 19. Recalling J.E. Rattenbury, *The Conversion of the Wesleys*, (London: Epworth, 1928), 216.

15   Telford, *Letters*, 8:145, 'To Walter Churchey', 20 June 1789.

a different matter to expect them to sing the complicated liturgical settings without the aid of a trained choir.

The Ordinal in the *Book of Common Prayer (1662)* began with a Preface in which was outlined the pattern of the threefold order of ministry, the testing of call and character of the candidates, and the required minimum ages for ordination to the various orders. John Wesley's Ordinal did not reproduce this Preface but began, without any introduction, with the modified title: *The Form and Manner of Making and Ordaining of Superintendants, Elders and Deacons.* [*sic*]

John Wesley retained the title 'deacon', although changed the character of the appointment. He disassociated the office from its restrictive appointment to a particular parish and made it a part of the itinerant ministry. However, following the established Anglican pattern, Wesley did not regard the order of deacon as being anything more than 'elders-in-training', having no place for the concept of a separate or permanent diaconal ministry.

In his revised rite for diaconal ordination, John Wesley changed the prayer book's phrase 'ordered' into 'ordained'. Indeed he did this throughout the Ordinal. In this revision, John Wesley could be seen following through his belief that as a presbyter he was of no different order from a bishop.[16] If a presbyter and bishop were of one order (*ordo*), although a bishop was of a higher degree (*gradus*), then, presumably, one could say the same for the relationship between deacon and presbyter and bishop. However, if it was Wesley's intention to reject the differentiation between orders, then he did not make all the changes necessary. In all three rites Wesley retained the collect which declared that Divine providence, or in the rite for elders and superintendants, the Holy Spirit 'hast appointed divers orders of ministers in thy church.'

After a shortened introductory rubric followed a much abbreviated presentation of the candidates for diaconal ordination, consisting of a simple reading of names, rather than the lengthy presentation formula of the Prayer Book. After the saying, not singing, of the Litany, the Service for Communion was begun with the special collect taken as in the Prayer Book rite. Unlike the Prayer Book though, John Wesley allowed no choice of epistle lection, providing only for the reading of 1 Timothy 3:8 and omitting the alternative from Acts 6:2. The epistle having been read, the examination began in the form as in the Prayer Book but with minor linguistic modifications. All references to ministry in the parochial context were broadened to emphasise the wider context of the itinerant ministry. It was, furthermore, suggested in Wesley's rite that it was always the work of a deacon to search for the 'sick, poor, and impotent, that they may be visited and relieved,' rather than the Prayer Book's limitation that it be required of them only 'where provision is so made.'

After the laying on of hands, the new deacons were, according to the Prayer Book, to be presented with a copy of the New Testament. Wesley changed this to require the giving of a whole Bible. Additionally, it was assumed that the

---

16   See the discussion of the influence of King and Stillingfleet above, page 39ff.

Methodist deacons would always be preachers, not only 'if thou be thereto licensed by the Bishop.' Reference to the deacons reading the homilies was removed in Wesley's revision.

Having been duly ordained, the deacons became eligible for ordination to office of elder. Wesley removed the final rubric from the rite, which limited such further ordination to only those who had spent one year in the diaconate.

Knowing that in the ancient church the terms priest, presbyter and elder were interchangeable, John Wesley substituted the title 'elder' wherever the *Book of Common Prayer (1662)* Ordinal referred to the office of priesthood. Although he had used the term 'priest' in his 1736 manuscript edition of Fleury's *Manners of the Ancient Christians*, Wesley replaced it with the term 'Minister' in his printed edition of 1789.[17]

Wesley's rite for the *Form and Manner of Ordaining Elders* followed that for the diaconate in having a much abbreviated presentation procedure. He made provision for the Gospel lesson to be from John 10:1, removing Matthew 9:36, which was offered as an alternative in the Prayer Book. After the examination of the ordinands, the *Veni Creator Spiritus* was to be said, not sung, in John Cosin's version. Cranmer's alternative version, which was printed in the Prayer Book along with Cosin's, was not offered by Wesley. The formula at the laying-on of hands was shortened by Wesley removing the reference from John 20:23 concerning the forgiving of sins. In common with other rites in the *Sunday Service*, Wesley removed the rubric directing the recitation of the Nicene Creed which, in the Prayer Book, followed the giving of the Bible.

The rites for the ordination of deacons and elders began after Morning Prayer and a sermon, the communion service commencing after the presentation of the ordinands. In the ordination of Superintendants the communion service began before the presentation, after Morning Prayer, a Sermon coming later in the rite.

Wesley allowed only one Epistle lection, that of Acts 20:17, omitting the alternative from 1 Timothy 3:1. He did, though, allow two of the Prayer Book's three alternatives for the Gospel. Wesley offered John 21:15 or Matthew 28:18, but removed the provision of John 20:19 which had been offered in the Prayer Book. Removing the Prayer Book's requirement for the Nicene Creed had the effect, in Wesley's rite, of placing the sermon immediately following the lessons. The sermon having been delivered, the *Sunday Service* began a very short presentation procedure; the Prayer Book's need for Royal oaths and mandates, along with oaths of obedience to the Archbishop, were swept away by Wesley. Perhaps there is a social statement being made in Wesley's modification of the presentation formula, the 'godly and well-learned man' offered in the Prayer Book is only a 'godly Man' in Wesley's revision.

---

17   See Ted A. Campbell, *John Wesley and Christian Antiquity*, 93–4 referring to Fleury, *Manners of the Ancient Christians*, John Wesley, ed. 3:8 (MS Colman 15:19; compare with 1798 ed. 12); 8:4 (Ms Colman 15:31; compare with 1798 ed, 23).

After returning the Litany to its form as supplied in the rite for diaconal ordination, rather than the modifications offered in the Prayer Book, there followed the examination of the candidate. As in the rite for the ordination of elders, John Cosin's form of the *Veni Creator Spiritus* was then to be said, not sung, Wesley again omitting Cranmer's alternative version.

Considering the revisions performed by John Wesley upon the Prayer Book Ordinal, there is in the ordination of Superintendants a curiosity. In the formula at the laying on of hands, John Wesley retained the words 'and remember that thou stir up the grace of God which is given thee by this imposition of our hands.' In his *Reply to the Roman Catechism*, John Wesley had claimed that ordination was not for the giving of grace, but was for the conveyance of ministerial commission.[18]

Wherever Wesley found the titles 'bishop' or 'Archbishop' in the *Book of Common Prayer (1662)* he replaced them with the title 'Superintendant'. Outler has suggested that Wesley's choice of this term reflects the administrative aspect of the office rather than an expression of 'anything approaching sacerdotal authority.'[19] Colin Williams has speculated that the changed titles of the presbyteral and episcopal ministers was symbolic of the fact that Wesley's ordinations for America 'were valid but irregular.'[20] It is, surely, unlikely that Williams' comment can stand up to scrutiny. There is no evidence to support a theory that John Wesley understood his ordinations to be 'valid but irregular.' He had no doubts at all about their validity or regularity. The ordinations he performed were both valid and regular, for validity and regularity were defined by himself.

An alternative thesis concerning the changes of ministerial titles can be put forward. Remembering that John Wesley ordained preachers who would be acting under his unique authority and direction, and also remembering that he was ordained presbyter, may throw further light upon his action. It was acceptable for Wesley to retain the order of deacon, as it was subordinate to his own order of presbyter, and so a fitting title for an assistant. It would be difficult for him to accept the order of presbyter as it would suggest an equality with himself, and bishop would suggest Wesley's inferiority. The titles elder and superintendant did not carry with them the traditional image of the established church authority, and so were acceptable, neutral, titles for positions which were still subject to the absolute authority of John Wesley. Additionally, there were social assumptions to be taken into consideration. At that time to be a bishop was to be a member of the ruling establishment – they lived in palaces and amassed great wealth – all highly unacceptable to the Methodist movement.

---

18   See above, page 48.

19   Albert C. Outler, *The Ordinal* in Dunkie and Quillan (eds), *Companion to the Book of Worship*, (Nashville: Abingdon, 1970), 113.

20   Colin Williams, *John Wesley's Theology Today*, (London: Epworth Press, 1960), 234.

This latter thesis gains strength when set alongside John Wesley's scathing letter sent to America when he discovered that Coke and Asbury had given themselves the title of 'Bishops'. He wrote to Asbury:

There is, indeed, a wide difference between the relation wherein you stand to the Americans and the relation wherein I stand to all the Methodists. You are the elder brother of the American Methodists: I am under God the father of the whole family ... But in one point, my dear brother, I am afraid both the Doctor and you differ from me. I study to be little: you study to be great. I creep: you strut along. I found a school: you a college! nay, and call it after your own names! O beware, do not seek to be something! Let me be nothing, and 'Christ be all in all!'

One instance of this, of your greatness, has given me great concern. How can you, how dare you suffer yourself to be called Bishop? I shudder, I start at the very thought! Men may call me a knave or a fool, a rascal, a scoundrel, and I am content; but they shall never by my consent call me a Bishop![21]

Edgar Thompson hints that this particular letter from Wesley to Asbury was written with 'tongue in cheek.' But the joke was not well received by Asbury, who took it as rebuke. Thompson has written that 'It is always dangerous to jest, when the jest has to be carried three thousand miles across the ocean. By the time it arrives the flavour of the humour has evaporated.'[22]

It is clear that John Wesley's understanding and exercise of authority over the Methodist societies, 'under God the father of the whole family,' is the crucial factor which must be considered in order to understand his intentions when appointing and ordaining preachers in his connexion. In his own opinion, and by his own words, ordination was not the giving of grace, but was for the conveyance of ministerial commission.[23]

Wesley remained convinced of the efficacy of the episcopalian model of church government. Theologically, he argued, he was a bishop, the scriptural episcopos, even though he had received no formal consecration. Furthermore, it can be asserted that Wesley's intention for the Methodists in America was that they should have an episcopal system of government. If he had not intended Coke to function as a bishop then he would not have needed to ordain him as a superintendant, for he was already a priest in the Church of England.

Wesley asserted that whilst presbyters and bishops are of the same order they have different functions. That John Wesley accepted and wished to continue this understanding can be asserted by the fact that the act of ordination itself was reserved for superintendants. But the superintendants would exercise a scriptural episcopacy.

---

21   Telford (ed.), *Letters*, 8:91 To Francis Asbury, 20 September 1788.

22   Edgar W. Thompson, *Wesley: Apostolic Man*, 67.

23   See above, page 48.

It can be seen that Wesley's Ordinal was a conservative adaptation of an existing text, rather than the creation of something new. John Wesley intended to retain and preserve as much of the *Book of Common Prayer (1662)* order as he could.

Chapter 8

The Text

Wesley's Adaptation of the Prayer Book Ordinal

WESLEY'S ADAPTATION

THE FORM AND MANNER OF MAKING AND ORDAINING OF SUPERINTENDANTS, ELDERS, AND DEACONS

PRAYER BOOK ORDINAL

THE FORM AND MANNER OF MAKING ORDAINING AND CONSECRATING OF BISHOPS, PRIESTS AND DEACONS ACCORDING TO THE ORDER OF THE CHURCH OF ENGLAND

THE PREFACE.

THE FORM AND MANNER OF MAKING OF DEACONS.

When the Day appointed by the Superintendant is come, after Morning Prayer is ended, there shall be a Sermon, or Exhortation, declaring the Duty and Office of such as come to be admitted Deacons.

After which one of the Elders shall present unto the Superintendant the Persons to be ordained Deacons: and their Names being read aloud, the Superintendant shall say unto the People:

THE FORM AND MANNER OF MAKING OF DEACONS.

When the Day appointed by the Bishop is come, after Morning Prayer is ended, there shall be a Sermon or Exhortation, declaring the Duty and Office of such as come to be admitted Deacons; how necessary that Order is in the Church of Christ, and also, how the people ought to esteem them in their Office.

First, the Archdeacon, or his Deputy, shall present unto the Bishop (sitting in his Chair, near to the holy Table) such as desire to be ordained Deacons, (each of them being decently habited,) saying these words,

Reverend Father in God, I present unto you these persons present, to be admitted Deacons.

The Bishop.

Take heed that the persons, whom ye present unto us, be apt and meet, for their learning and godly conversation, to exercise their Ministry duly, to the honour of God, and the edifying of his Church.

The Archdeacon shall answer,

I have enquired of them, and also examined them, and think them so to be.

Then the Bishop shall say unto the people:

Brethren, if there be any of you, who knoweth any impediment or crime in any of these persons presented to be ordained deacons, for the which he ought not to be admitted to that office, let him come forth in the Name of God, and shew what the crime or impediment is.

And if any Crime or Impediment be objected, the Superintendant shall surcease from ordaining that Person, until such Time as the Party accused shall be found clear of that Crime.

Then the Superintendant (commending such as shall be found meet to be ordained, to the Prayers of the Congregation) shall, with the Ministers and People present, say the Litany.

Then shall be said the Service for the Communion, with the Collect, Epistle, and Gospel, as followeth.

The Collect

Almighty God, who by thy Divine Providence hast appointed divers orders of ministers in thy church, and didst inspire thine apostles to choose into the order of deacons the first martyr saint Stephen, with others; Mercifully behold these thy servants now called to the like office and administration; replenish them so with the truth of thy doctrine, and adorn them with innocency of life, that both by word and good example they may faithfully serve thee in this office, to the glory of thy Name, and the edification of thy church, through the merits of our Saviour Jesus Christ, who liveth and reigneth with thee and the Holy Ghost, now and for ever. Amen.

The Epistle. 1 Tim. iii. 8.

Brethren, if there be any of you, who knoweth any impediment or notable crime, in any of these persons presented to be ordered deacons, for the which he ought not to be admitted to that Office, let him come forth in the Name of God, and shew what the Crime or Impediment is.

And if any great Crime or Impediment be objected, the Bishop shall surcease from Ordering that person, until such time as the party accused shall be found clear of that Crime.

Then the Bishop (commending such as shall be found meet to be Ordered, to the Prayers of the Congregation) shall, with the Clergy and People present, sing or say the Litany, with the Prayers, as followeth.

[The Litany and Suffrages are printed]

Then shall be sung or said the Service for the Communion, with the Collect, Epistle, and Gospel, as followeth.

The Collect

Almighty God, who by thy Divine Providence hast appointed divers Orders of Ministers in thy Church, and didst inspire thine Apostles to choose into the Order of Deacons the first Martyr Saint Stephen, with others; Mercifully behold these thy servants now called to the like Office and Administration; replenish them so with the truth of thy Doctrine, and adorn them with innocency of life, that both by word and good example they may faithfully serve thee in this Office, to the glory of thy Name, and the edification of thy Church, through the merits of our Saviour Jesus Christ, who liveth and reigneth with thee and the Holy Ghost, now and for ever. Amen.

The Epistle. 1 Tim. iii. 8. or Acts vi.2.

And before the Gospel, the Bishop sitting in his Chair, shall cause the Oath of the King's Supremacy, and against the power and authority of all foreign Potentates, to be ministered unto every one of them that are to be Ordered.

The Oath of the King's Sovereignty.

I A.B. do swear, that I do from my heart abhor, detest, and abjure, as impious and heretical, that damnable Doctrine and Position, that Princes excommunicated or deprived by the Pope, or any other Authority of the See of Rome, may be deposed or murdered by their subjects, or any other whatsoever. And I do declare, that no foreign Prince. Person, Prelate, State, or Potentate, hath, or ought to have, any jurisdiction, Power, Superiority, Preeminence, or Authority, Ecclesiastical or Spiritual, within this Realm. So help me God.

Then shall the Superintendant examine every one of them that are to be ordained, in the Presence of the People, after this manner following:

Do you trust that you are inwardly moved by the Holy Ghost to take upon you this office and ministration, to serve God for the promoting of his glory, and the edifying of his people?

Answer. I trust so.

The Superintendant.

Do you think that you are truly called, according to the will of our Lord Jesus Christ, to the ministry of the church? Answer. I think so.

The Superintendant.

Do you unfeignedly believe all the canonical Scriptures of the Old and New Testament?

Answer. I do believe them.

The Superintendant.

Will you diligently read the same unto the people whom you shall be appointed to serve?

Answer. I will.

The Superintendant.

It appertaineth to the office of a Deacon, to assist the elder in Divine Service, and especially when he ministereth the holy Communion, to help him in the distribution thereof, and to read and expound the holy Scriptures; to instruct the youth, and in the absence of the elder to baptise. And furthermore, it is his office, to search for the sick, poor, and

Then shall the Bishop examine every one of them that are to be Ordered, in the presence of the people, after this manner following.

Do you trust that you are inwardly moved by the Holy Ghost to take upon you this Office and Ministration, to serve God for the promoting of his glory, and the edifying of his people?

Answer. I trust so.

The Bishop.

Do you think that you are truly called, according to the will of our Lord Jesus Christ, and the due order of this Realm, to the Ministry of the Church?
Answer. I think so.

The Bishop.

Do you unfeignedly believe all the Canonical Scriptures of the Old and New Testament?

Answer. I do believe them.

The Bishop.

Will you diligently read the same unto the people assembled in the Church where you shall be appointed to serve?

Answer. I will.

The Bishop.

It appertaineth to the Office of a Deacon, in the Church where he shall be appointed to serve, to assist the Priest in Divine Service, and especially when he ministereth the holy Communion, to help him in the distribution thereof, and to read holy Scriptures and Homilies in the Church; to instruct the youth in the Catechism; in the absence of the Priest to

impotent, that they may be visited and relieved. Will you do this gladly and willingly?

Answer. I will do so, by the help of God.

The Superintendant.

Will you apply all your diligence to frame and fashion your own lives, and the lives of your families, according to the doctrine of Christ; and to make both yourself and them, as much as you lieth, wholesome examples of the flock of Christ?

Answer. I will so do, the Lord being my helper.

The Superintendant.

Will you reverently obey them to whom the charge and government over you is committed, following with a glad mind and will their godly admonitions? Answer. I will endeavour so to do, the Lord being my helper.

Then the Superintendant laying his Hands severally upon the Head of every one of them shall say,

Take thou authority to execute the office of a deacon in the church of God; In the Name of the Father, and of the Son, and of the Holy Ghost. Amen.

Then shall the Superintendant deliver to every one of them the Holy Bible, saying,

Take thou authority to read the holy Scriptures in the church of God, and to preach the same.

Then one of them appointed by the Superintendant shall read,

The Gospel. Luke, xii.35

baptize infants; and to preach, if he be admitted thereto by the Bishop. And furthermore, it is his office, where provision is so made, to search for the sick, poor, and impotent people of the Parish, to intimate their estates, names, and places where they dwell, unto the Curate, that by his exhortation they may be relieved with the alms of the Parishioners, or others. Will you do this gladly and willingly?

Answer. I will do so, by the help of God.

The Bishop.

Will you apply all your diligence to frame and fashion your own lives, and the lives of your families, according to the Doctrine of Christ; and to make both yourself and them, as much as you lieth, wholesome examples of the flock of Christ?

Answer. I will so do, the Lord being my helper.

The Bishop.

Will you reverently obey your Ordinary, and other chief Ministers of the Church, and them to whom the charge and government over you is committed, following with a glad mind and will their godly admonitions?

Answer. I will endeavour so to do, the Lord being my helper.

Then the Bishop laying his Hands severally upon the head of every one of them, humbly kneeling before him, shall say,

Take thou authority to execute the office of a Deacon in the Church of God committed unto thee; In the Name of the Father, and of the Son, and of the Holy Ghost. Amen.

The shall the Bishop deliver to every one of them the New Testament, saying,

Take thou authority to read the Gospel in the church of God, and to preach the same, if thou be thereto licensed by the Bishop himself.

Then one of them appointed by the Bishop, shall read,

The Gospel. Luke, xii.35

Then shall the Superintendant proceed in the Communion, and all that are ordained shall receive the Holy Communion.

The Communion ended, immediately before the Benediction, shall be said these Collects following:

Almighty God, giver of all good things, who of thy great goodness hast vouchsafed to accept and take these thy servants into the office of deacons in thy church; Make them, we beseech thee, O Lord, to be modest, humble, and constant in their ministration, and to have a ready will to observe all spiritual discipline; that they having always the testimony of a good conscience, and continuing ever stable and strong in thy Son Christ, may so well behave themselves in this inferior office, that they may be found worthy to be called unto the higher ministries in thy church, through the same thy Son our Saviour Jesus Christ; to whom be glory and honour world without end. Amen

Prevent us, O Lord, in all our doings with thy most gracious favour, and further us with thy continual help; that in all our works begun, continued, and ended in thee, we may glorify thy holy Name, and finally by thy mercy, obtain everlasting life, through Jesus Christ our Lord. Amen.

The peace of God, which passeth all understanding, keep your hearts and minds in the knowledge and love of God, and of his Son Jesus Christ our Lord. And the blessing of God almighty, the Father, the Son, and the Holy Ghost, be amongst you, and remain with you always. Amen

Then shall the Bishop proceed in the Communion, and all that are ordered shall tarry, and receive the Holy Communion the same day with the Bishop.

The Communion ended, after the last Collect, and immediately before the Benediction, shall be said these Collects following.

Almighty God, giver of all good things, who of thy great goodness hast vouchsafed to accept and take these thy servants unto the Office of Deacons in thy church; Make them, we beseech thee, O Lord, to be modest, humble, and constant in their Ministration; to have a ready will to observe all spiritual Discipline; that they having always the testimony of a good conscience, and continuing ever stable and strong in thy Son Christ, may so well behave themselves in this inferior office, that they may be found worthy to be called unto the higher Ministries in thy Church, through the same thy Son our Saviour Jesus Christ; to whom be glory and honour world without end. Amen

Prevent us, O Lord, in all our doings with thy most gracious favour, and further us with thy continual help; that in all our works, begun, continued, and ended in thee, we may glorify thy holy Name, and finally by thy mercy obtain everlasting life; through Jesus Christ our Lord. Amen.

The peace of God, which passeth all understanding, keep your hearts and minds in the knowledge and love of God, and of his Son Jesus Christ our Lord. And the blessing of God almighty, the Father, the Son, and the Holy Ghost, be amongst you, and remain with you always. Amen

And here it must be declared unto the Deacon, that he must continue in that Office of a Deacon the space of a whole year (except for reasonable causes it shall otherwise seem good unto the Bishop) to the intent he may be perfect, and well expert in the things appertaining to the Ecclesiastical Administration. In executing whereof if he be found faithful and diligent, he may be admitted by his Diocesan to the Order of Priesthood, at the times appointed in the Canon; or else, on urgent occasions, upon some other Sunday or Holy-Day, in the face of the Church, in such manner and form as hereafter followeth.

THE FORM AND MANNER OF ORDAINING OF ELDERS.

When the Day appointed by the Superintendant is come, after Morning Prayer is ended, there shall be a Sermon, or Exhortation, declaring the Duty and Office of such as come to be admitted Elders; how necessary that Order is in the Church of Christ, and also how the People ought to esteem them in their Office.

First, one of the Elders shall present unto the Superintendant all them that are to be ordained, and say,

I Present unto you these persons present, to be ordained Elders.

Then their Names being read aloud, the Superintendant shall say unto the People;

Good People, these are they whom we purpose, God willing, this day to ordain Elders. For after due examination, we find not to the contrary, but that they are lawfully called to this function and ministry, and that they are persons meet for the same. But if there be any of you, who knoweth any impediment or crime in any of them, for the which he ought not to be received into this holy ministry, let him come forth in the name of God, and shew what the crime or impediment is.

THE FORM AND MANNER OF ORDAINING OF PRIESTS.

When the Day appointed by the Bishop is come; after Morning Prayer is ended, there shall be a Sermon or Exhortation, declaring the Duty and Office of such as come to be admitted Priests; how necessary that Order is in the Church of Christ; and also how the People ought to esteem them in their Office.

First, the Archdeacon, or, in his absence, one appointed in his stead, shall present unto the Bishop (sitting in his Chair, near the holy Table) all them that shall receive the Order of Priesthood that day; (each of them being decently habited;) and say,

Reverend Father in God, I Present unto you these persons present, to be admitted to the Order of Priesthood.

The Bishop.

Take heed that the persons, whom ye present to us, be apt and meet, for the learning and godly conversation, to exercise their ministry duly, to the honour of God, and the edifying of his Church.

The Archdeacon shall answer,

I have enquired of them, and also examined them; and think them so to be.

Then the Bishop shall say unto the people:

Good People, these are they whom we purpose, God willing, to receive this day unto the holy office of Priesthood: For after due examination, we find not to the contrary, but that they are lawfully called to their Function and Ministry, and that they be persons meet for the same. But if there be any of you, who knoweth any impediment or notable crime in any of them, for the which he ought not to be received into this holy ministry, let him come forth in the Name of God, and shew

And if any Crime or Impediment be objected, the Superintendant shall surcease from ordaining that Person, until such Time as the Party accused shall be found clear of that Crime.

Then the Superintendant (commending such as shall be found meet to be ordained, to the Prayers of the Congregation) shall, with the Ministers and People present, say the Litany, as is before appointed in the Form of Ordaining Deacons, omitting the last Prayer, and the Blessing.

Then shall be said the Service for the Communion; with the Collect, Epistle, and Gospel, as followeth.

Almighty God, giver of all good things, who by thy holy Spirit hast appointed divers orders of ministers in thy church; mercifully behold these thy servants now called to the office of Elders; and replenish them so with the truth of thy doctrine, and adorn them with innocency of life, that both by word and good example they may faithfully serve thee in this office, to the glory of thy name, and the edification of thy church, through the merits of our Saviour, Jesus Christ, who liveth and reigneth, with thee and the Holy Ghost, world without end. Amen.

The Epistle. Ephesians iv.7.

After this shall be read for the Gospel, part of the Tenth Chapter of Saint John

And that done, the Superintendant shall say unto them as hereafter followeth,

---

what the Crime or Impediment is.

And if any great Crime or Impediment be objected, the Bishop shall surcease from Ordering that Person, until such time as the party accused shall be found clear of that Crime.

Then the Bishop (commending such as shall be found meet to be Ordered, to the Prayers of the Congregation) shall, with the Clergy and People present, sing or say the Litany, with the Prayers, as is before appointed in the Form of Ordering Deacons; save only, that, in the proper Suffrage there added, the word [Deacons] shall be omitted, and the word [Priests] inserted instead of it.

Then shall be sung or said the Service for the Communion; with the Collect, Epistle, and Gospel, as followeth.

Almighty God, giver of all good things, who by thy holy Spirit hast appointed divers Orders of Ministers in thy Church; mercifully behold these thy servants now called to the Office of Priesthood; and replenish them so with the truth of thy doctrine, and adorn them with innocency of life, that both by word and good example they may faithfully serve thee in this Office, to the glory of thy name, and the edification of thy church, through the merits of our Saviour, Jesus Christ, who liveth and reigneth, with thee and the Holy Ghost, world without end. Amen.

The Epistle. Ephesians iv.7.

After this shall be read for the Gospel, part of the ninth chapter of Saint Matthew, as followeth.

S. Matth. 9.36.

Or else this that followeth, out of the tenth chapter of Saint John.
S. John 10.1.

Then the Bishop, sitting in his chair, shall minister unto every one of them the Oath concerning the King's Supremacy, as it is before set forth in the Form for the Ordering of Deacons

And that being done, he shall say unto them as hereafter followeth,

You have heard, brethren, as well in your private examination, as in the exhortation which was now made to you, and in the holy lessons taken out of the Gospel, and the writings of the Apostles, of what dignity, and of how great importance this office is, whereunto ye are called. And now again we exhort you in the name of our Lord Jesus Christ, that you have in remembrance, into how high a dignity, and to how weighty an office and charge ye are called: That is to say, to be Messengers, watchmen, and stewards of the Lord; to teach, and to premonish, to feed and provide for the Lord's family; to seek for Christ's sheep that are dispersed abroad, and for his children who are in the midst of this naughty world, that they may be saved through Christ for ever.

Have always therefore printed in your remembrance, how great a treasure is committed to your charge. For they are the sheep of Christ, which he bought with his death, and for whom he shed his blood. The church and congregation whom you must serve, is his Spouse, and his body. And if it shall happen, the same church, or any member thereof do take any hurt or hindrance by reason of your negligence, ye know the greatness of the fault, and also the horrible punishment that will ensue. Wherefore consider with yourselves the end of the ministry towards the children of God, towards the spouse and body of Christ; and see that you never cease your labour, your care and diligence, until you have done all that lieth in you, according to your bounden duty, to bring all such as are or shall be committed to your charge, unto that agreement in the faith and knowledge of God, and to that ripeness and perfectness of age in Christ, that there be no place left among you, either for error in religion, or viciousness in life.

Forasmuch then as your office is both of so great excellency, and of so great difficulty, ye see with how great care and study ye ought to apply yourselves, as well that ye may shew yourselves dutiful and

You have heard, brethren, as well in your private examination, as in the exhortation which was now made to you, and in the holy Lessons taken out of the Gospel, and the writings of the Apostles, of what dignity, and of how great importance this Office is, whereunto ye are called. And now again we exhort you in the name of our Lord Jesus Christ, that you have in remembrance, into how high a dignity, and to how weighty an Office and charge ye are called: That is to say, to be Messengers, Watchmen, and Stewards of the Lord; to teach, and to premonish, to feed and provide for the Lord's family; to seek for Christ's sheep that are dispersed abroad, and for his children who are in the midst of this naughty world, that they may be saved through Christ for ever.

Have always therefore printed in your remembrance, how great a treasure is committed to your charge. For they are the sheep of Christ, which he bought with his death, and for whom he shed his blood. The Church and Congregation whom you must serve, is his Spouse, and his Body. And if it shall happen, the same Church, or any Member thereof do take any hurt or hindrance by reason of your negligence, ye know the greatness of the fault, and also the horrible punishment that will ensue. Wherefore consider with yourselves the end of the ministry towards the children of God, towards the spouse and body of Christ; and see that you never cease your labour, your care and diligence, until you have done all that lieth in you, according to your bounden duty, to bring all such as are or shall be committed to your charge, unto that agreement in the faith and knowledge of God, and to that ripeness and perfectness of age in Christ, that there be no place left among you, either for error in religion, or viciousness in life.

Forasmuch then as your Office is both of so great excellency, and of so great difficulty, ye see with how great care and study ye ought to apply yourselves, as well that ye may shew yourselves dutiful and thankful unto that Lord, who hath placed you in so high a dignity; as also to beware that neither you yourselves offend, nor be occasion that others offend. Howbeit ye cannot have a mind and will thereto of yourselves; for that will and ability is given of God alone: therefore ye ought, and have need to pray earnestly for his holy Spirit. And seeing that you cannot by any other means compass the doing of so weighty a work, pertaining to the salvation of man, but with doctrine and exhortation taken out of the Holy Scriptures, and with a life agreeable to the same: consider how studious ye ought to be in reading and learning the Scriptures, and in framing the manners both of yourselves, and of them that specially pertain unto you, according to the rule of the same Scriptures: and for this self-same cause, how ye ought to forsake and set aside (as much as you may) all worldly cares and studies.

We have good hope that you have all weighed and pondered these things with yourselves long before this time; and that you have clearly determined, by God's grace, to give yourselves wholly to this office, whereunto it hath pleased God to call you: so that, as much as lieth in you, you will apply yourselves wholly to this one thing, and draw all your cares and studies this way, and that you will continually pray to God the Father, by the mediation of our only Saviour Jesus Christ, for the heavenly assistance of the Holy Ghost; that by daily reading and weighing of the Scriptures, ye may wax riper and stronger in your ministry; and that ye may so endeavour yourselves from time to time to sanctify the lives of you and your's, and to fashion them after the rule and doctrine of Christ, that ye may be wholesome and godly examples and patterns for the people to follow.

And now that this present congregation of Christ, here assembled, may also understand your minds and wills in these things, and that this your promise may the more move you to do your duties; ye shall answer plainly to these things, which we,

thankful unto that Lord, who hath placed you in so high a dignity; as also to beware that neither you yourselves offend, nor be occasion that others offend. Howbeit ye cannot have a mind and will thereto of yourselves; for that will and ability is given of God alone: therefore ye ought, and have need to pray earnestly for his holy Spirit. And seeing that you cannot by any other means compass the doing of so weighty a work, pertaining to the salvation of man, but with doctrine and exhortation taken out of the Holy Scriptures, and with a life agreeable to the same: consider how studious ye ought to be in reading and learning the Scriptures, and in framing the manners both of yourselves, and of them that specially pertain unto you, according to the rule of the same Scriptures: and for this self-same cause, how ye ought to forsake and set aside (as much as you may) all worldly cares and studies.

We have good hope that you have all weighed and pondered these things with yourselves long before this time; and that you have clearly determined, by God's grace, to give yourselves wholly to this office, whereunto it hath pleased God to call you: so that, as much as lieth in you, you will apply yourselves wholly to this one thing, and draw all your cares and studies this way, and that you will continually pray to God the Father, by the mediation of our only Saviour Jesus Christ, for the heavenly assistance of the Holy Ghost; that by daily reading and weighing of the Scriptures, ye may wax riper and stronger in your ministry; and that ye may so endeavour yourselves from time to time to sanctify the lives of you and your's, and to fashion them after the rule and doctrine of Christ, that ye may be wholesome and godly examples and patterns for the people to follow.

And now that this present Congregation of Christ, here assembled, may also understand your minds and wills in these things, and that this your promise may the more move you to do your duties; ye shall answer plainly to these things, which we, in the Name of God, and of his Church, shall demand of you touching the same.

Do you think in your heart, that you are truly called, according to the will of our Lord Jesus Christ, to the order of Elders.

Answer. I think so.

The Superintendant.

Are you persuaded that the Holy Scriptures contain sufficiently all doctrine required of necessity for eternal salvation through faith in Jesus Christ? And are you determined, out of the said Scriptures to instruct the people committed to your charge, and to teach nothing, as required of necessity to eternal salvation, but that which you shall be persuaded, may be concluded and proved by the Scripture?

Answer. I am so persuaded, and have so determined, by God's grace.

The Superintendant.

Will you then give your faithful diligence, always so to minister the doctrine and sacraments, and the discipline of Christ, as the Lord hath commanded.

Answer. I will so do, by the help of the Lord.

The Superintendant.

Will you be ready with all faithful diligence to banish and drive away all erroneous and strange doctrines contrary to God's word; and to use both public and private monitions and exhortations, as well to the sick as to the whole within your district, as need shall require, and occasion shall be given?

Answer. I will, the Lord being my helper.

The Superintendant.

Will you be diligent in prayers, and in reading of the holy Scriptures, and in such studies as help to the knowledge of the same, laying aside the study of the world

in the Name of God, and of his Church, shall demand of you touching the same.

Do you think in your heart, that you are truly called, according to the will of our Lord Jesus Christ, and the order of this Church of England, to the Order and Ministry of Priesthood?

Answer. I think it.

The Bishop.

Are you persuaded that the Holy Scriptures contain sufficiently all Doctrine required of necessity for eternal salvation through faith in Jesus Christ? And are you determined, out of the said Scriptures to instruct the people committed to your charge, and to teach nothing, as required of necessity to eternal salvation, but that which you shall be persuaded, may be concluded and proved by the Scripture?

Answer. I am so persuaded, and have so determined, by God's grace.

The Bishop.

Will you then give your faithful diligence, always so to minister the Doctrine and Sacraments, and the discipline of Christ, as the Lord hath commanded, and as this Church and Realm hath received the same, according to the commandments of God; so that you may teach the people committed to your cure and charge with all diligence to keep and observe the same?

Answer. I will so do, by the help of the Lord.

The Bishop.

Will you be ready with all faithful diligence to banish and drive away all erroneous and strange doctrines contrary to God's word; and to use both publick and private monitions and exhortations, as well to the sick as to the whole within your cures, as need shall require, and occasion shall be given?

Answer. I will, the Lord being my helper.

The Bishop.

Will you be diligent in prayers, and in reading of the holy Scriptures, and in such studies as help to the knowledge of the same, laying aside the study of the world and the flesh.

Answer. I will endeavour so to do, the Lord being my helper.

The Superintendant.

Will you be diligent to frame and fashion your own selves, and your families, according to the doctrine of Christ; and to make both yourselves and them, as much as in you lieth, wholesome examples and patterns to the flock of Christ?

Answer. I shall apply myself thereto, the Lord being my helper.

The Superintendant.

Will you maintain and set forwards, as much as lieth in you, quietness, peace and love among all Christian people, and especially among them that are or shall be committed to your charge?

Answer. I will do so, the Lord being my helper.

The Superintendant.

Will you reverently obey your chief ministers, unto whom is committed the charge and government over you; following with a glad mind and will their godly admonitions, and submitting yourselves to their godly judgements?

Answer. I will do so, the Lord being my helper.

Then shall the Superintendant standing up, say,

Almighty God, who hath given you this will to do all these things; grant also unto you strength and power to perform the same; that he may accomplish his work which he hath begun in you, through Jesus Christ our Lord. Amen

After this the Congregation shall be desired, secretly in their Prayers, to make their humble Supplications to God for all these Things: for the which Prayers there shall be Silence kept for a space.

After which shall be said by the Superintendant (the persons to be ordained Elders, all kneeling) Veni, Creator, Spiritus; the Superintendant beginning, and the Elders and others that are present

and the flesh.

Answer. I will endeavour myself so to do, the Lord being my helper.

The Bishop.

Will you be diligent to frame and fashion your own selves, and your families, according to the doctrine of Christ; and to make both yourselves and them, as much as in you lieth, wholesome examples and patterns to the flock of Christ?

Answer. I shall apply myself thereto, the Lord being my helper.

The Bishop.

Will you maintain and set forwards, as much as lieth in you, quietness, peace and love among all Christian people, and especially among them that are or shall be committed to your charge?

Answer. I will do so, the Lord being my helper.

The Bishop.

Will you reverently obey your Ordinary and other chief Ministers, unto whom is committed the charge and government over you; following with a glad mind and will their godly admonitions, and submitting yourselves to their godly judgements?

Answer. I will do so, the Lord being my helper.

Then shall the Bishop, standing up, say,

Almighty God, who hath given you this will to do all these things; Grant also unto you strength and power to perform the same; that he may accomplish his work which he hath begun in you, through Jesus Christ our Lord. Amen

After this the Congregation shall be desired, secretly in their Prayers, to make their humble Supplications to God for all these Things: for the which Prayers there shall be silence kept for a space.

After which shall be sung or said by the Bishop (the persons to be ordained Priests, all kneeling) Veni, Creator, Spiritus; the Bishop beginning, and the Priests and others that are present answering by answering by Verses, as followeth.

Come, Holy Ghost, our Souls inspire,
And lighten with celestial fire.
Thou the anointing Spirit art,
Who dost thy sev'nfold gifts impart:
Thy blessed Unction from above,
Is comfort, life, and fire of love.
Enable with perpetual light,
The dullness of our blinded sight:
Anoint and cheer our soiled face
With the abundance of thy grace:
Keep far our foes, give peace at home;
Where thou art guide no ill can come.
Teach us to know the Father, Son,
And thee of both, to be but one:
That through the ages all along,
This may be our endless Song;
Praise to thy eternal merit,
Father, Son, and Holy Spirit.

That done, the Superintendant shall pray in this wise, and say,

Let us pray.

Almighty God, and heavenly Father, who of thine infinite love and goodness towards us, hast given to us thy only and most dearly beloved Son Jesus Christ to be our Redeemer, and the Author of everlasting life; who after he had made perfect our redemption by his death, and was ascended into heaven, sent abroad into the world his Apostles, Prophets, Evangelists, Doctors, and Pastors; by whose labour and ministry he gathered together a great flock in all parts of the world, to set forth the eternal praise of thy holy Name: for these so great benefits of thy eternal goodness, and for that thou hast vouchsafed to call these thy servants here present to the same Office and Ministry appointed for the salvation of mankind, we render unto thee most hearty thanks, we praise and worship thee; and we humbly beseech thee by the same the blessed Son, to grant unto all, who either here or elsewhere call upon thy holy Name, that we may continue to shew ourselves thankful unto thee for these and all other

Verses, as followeth.

Come, Holy Ghost, our Souls inspire,
And lighten with celestial fire.
Thou the anointing Spirit art,
Who dost thy sev'nfold gifts impart:
Thy blessed Unction from above,
Is comfort, life, and fire of love.
Enable with perpetual light,
The dullness of our blinded sight:
Anoint and cheer our soiled face
With the abundance of thy grace:
Keep far our foes, give peace at home;
Where thou art guide no ill can come.
Teach us to know the Father, Son,
And thee of both, to be but one:
That through the ages all along,
This may be our endless Song;
Praise to thy eternal merit,
Father, Son, and Holy Spirit.

Or this:

[Cranmer's alternative form of *Veni Creator Spiritus*]

That done, the Bishop shall pray in this wise, and say,

Let us pray.

Almighty God, and heavenly Father, who of thine infinite love and goodness towards us, hast given to us thy only and most dearly beloved Son Jesus Christ to be our Redeemer, and the Author of everlasting life; who after he had made perfect our redemption by his death, and was ascended into heaven, sent abroad into the world his Apostles, Prophets, Evangelists, Doctors, and Pastors; by whose labour and ministry he gathered together a great flock in all parts of the world, to set forth the eternal praise of thy holy Name: for these so great benefits of thy eternal goodness, and for that thou hast vouchsafed to call these thy servants here present to the same Office and Ministry appointed for the salvation of mankind, we render unto thee most hearty thanks, we praise and worship thee; and we humbly beseech thee by the same the blessed Son, to grant unto all, which either here or elsewhere call upon thy holy Name, that we may continue to shew ourselves thankful unto thee for these and all other thy benefits; and that we may daily increase and go forwards in the knowledge and faith of thee and thy Son by the Holy Spirit. So that as well by these thy Ministers, as by them over whom they shall be appointed thy Ministers, thy holy Name may be for ever glorified, and thy blessed kingdom enlarged, through the same thy Son Jesus Christ our Lord; who livest and reigneth with thee in the unity of the same Holy Spirit, world without end. Amen.

When this Prayer is done, the Superintendant, with the Elders present, shall lay their hands severally upon the Head of every one that received the order of Elders: the Receivers humbly kneeling upon their knees, and the Superintendant saying,

Receive the Holy Ghost for the Office and Work of an Elder in the Church of God, now committed unto thee by the imposition of our hands. And be thou a faithful Dispenser of the Word of God, and of his holy Sacraments; in the Name of the Father, and of the Son, and of the Holy Ghost. Amen.

Then the Superintendant shall deliver to every one of them, kneeling, the Bible into his hand, saying,

Take thou authority to preach the Word of God, and to administer the holy Sacraments in the Congregation.

When this is done, the Superintendant shall go on in the Service of the Communion, which all they that receive Orders shall take together.

The Communion being done, after the last Collect, and immediately before the Benediction, shall be said these collects.

Most merciful Father, we beseech thee to send upon these thy servants thy heavenly

---

thy benefits; and that we may daily increase and go forwards in the knowledge and faith of thee and thy Son by the Holy Spirit. So that as well by these thy Ministers, as by them over whom they shall be appointed thy Ministers, thy holy Name may be for ever glorified, and thy blessed kingdom enlarged, through the same thy Son Jesus Christ our Lord; who livest and reigneth with thee in the unity of the same Holy Spirit, world without end. Amen.

When this Prayer is done, the Bishop, with the Priests present, shall lay their hands severally upon the Head of every one that receiveth the Order of Priesthood : the receivers humbly kneeling upon their knees, and the Bishop saying,

Receive the Holy Ghost for the Office and work of a Priest in the Church of God, now committed unto thee by the Imposition of our hands. Whose sins thou dost forgive, they are forgiven; and whose sins thou dost retain, they are retained. And be thou a faithful Dispenser of the Word of God, and of his holy Sacraments; in the Name of the Father, and of the Son, and of the Holy Ghost. Amen.

Then the Bishop shall deliver to every one of them, kneeling, the Bible into his hand, saying,

Take thou authority to preach the Word of God, and to administer the holy Sacraments in the Congregation, where thou shalt be lawfully appointed thereunto.

When this is done, the Nicene Creed, shall be sung or said; and the Bishop shall after that go on in the Service of the Communion, which all they that receive Orders shall take together, and remain in the same place where hands were laid upon them, until such time as they have received the Communion.

The Communion being done, after the last Collect, and immediately before the Benediction, shall be said these collects.

Most merciful Father, we beseech thee to send upon these thy servants thy heavenly blessing; that they may be clothed with righteousness, and thy Word spoken by their mouths, may have such success, that it may never be spoken in vain. Grant also, that we may have grace to hear and receive what they shall deliver out of thy most holy Word, or agreeable to the same, as the means of our Salvation; that in all our words and deeds we may seek thy glory, and the increase of thy Kingdom, through Jesus Christ our Lord. Amen.

Prevent us, O Lord, in all our doings with thy most gracious favour, and further us with thy continual help; that in all our works begun, continued, and ended in thee, we may glorify thy holy Name, and finally by thy mercy, obtain everlasting life, through Jesus Christ our Lord. Amen.

The peace of God, which passeth all understanding, keep your hearts and minds in the knowledge and love of God, and of his Son Jesus Christ our Lord. And the blessing of God almighty, the Father, the Son, and the Holy Ghost, be amongst you, and remain with you always. Amen.

And if on the same day the Order of Deacons be given to some, and that of Elders to others; the Deacons shall be first presented, and then the Elders; and it shall suffice that the Litany be once said for both. The Collects shall both be used; first, that for Deacons, then that for Elders. The Epistle shall be Ephesians iv.4. to 13. as before in this Office. Immediately after which, they that are to be ordained Deacons shall be examined, and ordained, as is above prescribed. Then one of them having read the Gospel, which shall be St. John, x.1. as before in this Office; they that are to be ordained Elders, shall likewise be examined and ordained as is in this Office before appointed.

blessing; that they may be clothed with righteousness, and thy Word spoken by their mouths, may have such success, that it may never be spoken in vain. Grant also, that we may have grace to hear and receive what they shall deliver out of thy most holy Word, or agreeable to the same, as the means of our Salvation; that in all our words and deeds we may seek thy glory, and the increase of thy Kingdom, through Jesus Christ our Lord. Amen.

Prevent us, O Lord, in all our doings with thy most gracious favour, and further us with thy continual help; that in all our works, begun, continued, and ended in thee, we may glorify thy holy Name, and finally by thy mercy obtain everlasting life; through Jesus Christ our Lord. Amen.

The peace of God, which passeth all understanding, keep your hearts and minds in the knowledge and love of God, and of his Son Jesus Christ our Lord. And the blessing of God almighty, the Father, the Son, and the Holy Ghost, be amongst you and remain with you always. Amen.

And if on the same day the Order of Deacons be given to some, and the Order of Priesthood to others; the Deacons shall be first presented, and then the Priests; and it shall suffice that the Litany be once said for both. The Collects shall both be used; first, that for Deacons, then that for Priests. The Epistle shall be Ephesians iv.7 to 13 as before in this Office. Immediately after which, they that are to be made Deacons shall take the Oath of Supremacy, be examined, and Ordained, as is above prescribed. Then one of them having read the Gospel, (which shall be either out of S. Matth. 9.36–8, as before in this Office; or else S. Luke 12.35–8, as before in the Form for the Ordering of Deacons,) they that are to be made Priests, shall likewise take the Oath of Supremacy, be examined and Ordained, as is in this Office before appointed.

THE FORM OF ORDAINING OF A SUPERINTENDANT.	*THE FORM OF ORDAINING OR CONSECRATING OF AN ARCHBISHOP OR BISHOP WHICH IS ALWAYS TO BE PERFORMED UPON SOME SUNDAY OR HOLY-DAY*
After Morning Prayer is ended, the Superintendant shall begin the Communion Service; in which this shall be	When all things are duly prepared in the Church, and set in order; after Morning Prayer is ended, the Archbishop (or some other Bishop appointed) shall begin the Communion Service; in which this shall be
The Collect	The Collect
Almighty God, who by thy Son Jesus Christ didst give to thy holy apostles many excellent gifts, and didst charge them to feed thy flock; give grace, we beseech thee, to all the Ministers and Pastors of thy Church, that they may diligently preach thy Word, and duly administer the godly Discipline thereof'; and grant to the people that they may obediently follow the same; that all may receive the crown of everlasting glory, through Jesus Christ our Lord. Amen.	Almighty God, who by thy Son Jesus Christ didst give to thy holy Apostles many excellent gifts, and didst charge them to feed thy flock: Give grace, we beseech thee, to all the Bishops, the Pastors of thy Church, that they may diligently preach thy Word, and duly administer the godly discipline thereof'; and grant to the people, that they may obediently follow the same; that all may receive the crown of everlasting glory, through Jesus Christ our Lord. Amen.
Then shall be read by one of the Elders, the Epistle. Acts, xx.17.	And another Bishop shall read the Epistle. 1 St. Tim. 3.1. or this. For the Epistle. Acts 20.17.
Then another Elder shall read, The Gospel, St. John, xxi.15 or this: St. Matthew xxviii.18.	Then another Bishop shall read The Gospel. St. John 21.15 or else this. St. John 20.19 or this. St. Matth. 28.18.
After the Gospel and the Sermon are ended, the elected Person shall be presented by two Elders unto the Superintendant, saying,	After the Gospel, and the Nicene Creed, and the Sermon are ended, the elected Bishop (vested with his Rochet) shall be presented by two Bishops unto the Archbishop of that Province, (or to some other Bishop appointed by lawful commission,) the Archbishop sitting in his Chair, near the holy Table, and the Bishops that present him saying,
We present unto you this godly Man to be ordained a Superintendant.	Most reverend Father in God, we present unto you this godly and well-learned man to be Ordained and Consecrated Bishop.
	Then shall the Archbishop demand the King's mandate for the Consecration, and cause it to be read. And the Oath touching the acknowledgement of the King's Supremacy, shall be ministered to the persons elected, as it is set down in the Form for the Ordering of Deacons. And then shall be ministered unto them the

The Superintendant shall move the Congregation present to pray, saying thus to them:

Brethren, it is written in the Gospel of Saint Luke, That our Saviour Christ continued the whole night in prayer, before he did choose and send forth his twelve Apostles. It is written also in the acts of the Apostles, That the Disciples who were at Antioch, did fast and pray, before they laid hands on Paul and Barnabas, and sent them forth. Let us therefore, following the example of our Saviour Christ, and his Apostles, first fall to Prayer before we admit, and send forth this person presented unto us, to the work, whereunto we trust the Holy Ghost hath called him.

And then shall be said the Litany, as before, in the Form of Ordaining Deacons.

Then shall be said this Prayer following.

Almighty God, giver of all good things, who by thy Holy Spirit hast appointed divers orders of ministers in thy church;

Oath of due Obedience to the Archbishop, as followeth.

The Oath of Due obedience to the Archbishop

In the Name of God, Amen. I N. chosen Bishop of the Church and See of N. do profess and promise all due reverence and obedience to the Archbishop and to the Metropolitan Church of N. and to their Successors: So help me God, through Jesus Christ.

This oath shall not be made at the Consecration of an Archbishop.

Then the Archbishop shall move the Congregation present to pray, saying thus to them:

Brethren, it is written in the Gospel of Saint Luke, That our Saviour Christ continued the whole night in prayer, before he did choose and send forth his twelve Apostles. It is written also in the acts of the Apostles, That the Disciples who were at Antioch, did fast and pray, before they laid hands on Paul and Barnabas, and sent them forth. Let us therefore, following the example of our Saviour Christ and his Apostles, first fall to Prayer before we admit, and send forth this person presented unto us, to the work whereunto we trust the Holy Ghost hath called him.

And then shall be said the Litany, as before, in the Form of Ordering Deacons, save only that after this place, That it may please thee to illuminate all Bishops, &c. the proper Suffrage there following shall be omitted and this inserted instead of it;

That it may please thee to bless this our Brother elected, and to send thy grace upon him, that he may duly execute the office whereunto he is called, to the edifying of thy Church, and to the honour, praise and glory of thy Name, Answer. We beseech thee to hear us, good Lord.

Then shall be said this Prayer following.

Almighty God, giver of all good things, who by thy Holy Spirit hast appointed divers Orders of Ministers in thy Church:

mercifully behold this thy servant now called to the work and ministry of a Superintendant, and replenish him so with the truth of thy doctrine, and adorn him with innocency of life, that, both by word and deed, he may faithfully serve thee in this office, to the glory of thy Name and the edifying and well-governing of thy church, through the merits of our Saviour Jesus Christ, who liveth and reigneth with thee and the Holy Ghost, world without end. Amen.

Then the Superintendant shall say to him that is to be ordained,

Brother, forasmuch as the holy Scripture commands that we should not be hasty in laying on hands, and admitting any person to government in the church of Christ, which he hath purchased with no less price than the effusion of his own blood; before I admit you to this administration I will examine you on certain articles, to the end that the congregation present may have a trial, and bear witness how you are minded to behave yourself in the church of God.

Are you persuaded that you are truly called to this ministration, according to the will of our Lord Jesus Christ?

Answer. I am so persuaded.

The Superintendant.

Are you persuaded that the holy Scriptures contain sufficiently all doctrine required of necessity for eternal salvation, through faith in Jesus Christ? And are you determined out of the same holy Scriptures to instruct the people committed to your charge, and to teach or maintain nothing as required of necessity to eternal salvation, but that which you shall be persuaded may be concluded and proved by the same. Answer. I am persuaded, and determined by God's grace.

The Superintendant.

Will you then faithfully exercise yourself in the same holy Scriptures, and call upon God by prayer for the true understanding of the same, so as you may be able by

Mercifully behold this thy servant now called to the work and ministry of a Bishop; and replenish him so with the truth of thy doctrine, and adorn him with innocency of life, that, both by word and deed, he may faithfully serve thee in this office, to the glory of thy Name and the edifying and well-governing of thy Church, through the merits of our Saviour Jesus Christ, who liveth and reigneth with thee and the Holy Ghost, world without end. Amen.

Then the Archbishop, sitting in his Chair, shall say to him that is to be Consecrated,

Brother, forasmuch as the holy Scripture and the ancient Canons command that we should not be hasty in laying on hands, and admitting any person to Government in the Church of Christ, which he hath purchased with no less price than the effusion of his own blood: Before I admit you to this administration, I will examine you in certain articles, to the end that the Congregation present may have a trial, and bear witness, how you are minded to behave yourself in the Church of God.

Are you persuaded that you are truly called to this Ministration, according to the will of our Lord Jesus Christ, and order of this Realm?

Answer. I am so persuaded.

The Archbishop.

Are you persuaded that the holy Scriptures contain sufficiently all doctrine required of necessity for eternal salvation, through faith in Jesus Christ? And are you determined out of the same holy Scriptures to instruct the people committed to your charge, and to teach or maintain nothing as required of necessity to eternal salvation, but that which you shall be persuaded may be concluded and proved by the same. Answer. I am so persuaded, and determined, by God's grace.

The Archbishop.

Will you then faithfully exercise yourself in the same holy Scriptures, and call upon God by prayer, for the true understanding of the same; so as you may be able by them to teach and exhort with wholesome doctrine, and to withstand and convince the gainsayers?

Answer. I will so do, by the help of God.

The Superintendant.

Are you ready, and with faithful diligence, to banish and drive away all erroneous and strange doctrines contrary to God's word, and both privately and openly call upon and encourage others to the same?

Answer. I am ready, the Lord being my helper.

The Superintendant.

Will you deny all ungodliness and worldly lusts, and live soberly, righteously, and godly in this present world, that you may shew yourself in all things an example of good works unto others, that the adversary may be ashamed, having nothing to say against you?

Answer. I will so do, the Lord being my helper.

The Superintendant.

Will you maintain and set forward, as much as shall lie in you, quietness, love, and peace among all men; and such as shall be unquiet, disobedient, and criminal within your district, correct and punish, according to such authority as you have by God's Word, and as shall be committed unto you.

Answer. I will so do, by the help of God.

The Superintendant.

Will you be faithful in ordaining, sending, or laying hands upon others?

Answer. I will so be, by the help of God.

The Superintendant.

Will you shew yourself gentle, and merciful, for Christ's sake, to poor and needy people, and to all strangers destitute of help?

Answer. I will so shew myself, by God's help.

Then the Superintendant shall say,

Almighty God, our heavenly Father, who hath given you a good will to do all these

them to teach and exhort with wholesome doctrine, and to withstand and convince the gainsayers?

Answer. I will so do, by the help of God.

The Archbishop.

Are you ready, and with faithful diligence, to banish and drive away all erroneous and strange doctrines contrary to God's word; and both privately and openly to call upon and encourage others to the same?

Answer. I am ready, the Lord being my helper.

The Archbishop.

Will you deny all ungodliness and worldly lusts, and live soberly, righteously, and godly in this present world, that you may shew yourself in all things an example of good works unto others, that the adversary may be ashamed, having nothing to say against you?

Answer. I will so do, the Lord being my helper.

The Archbishop.

Will you maintain and set forward (as much as shall lie in you) quietness, peace, and love among all men; and such as shall be unquiet, disobedient, and criminous within your Diocese, correct and punish, according to such authority as you have by God's Word, and as shall be committed unto you by the Ordinance of this Realm?

Answer. I will so do, by the help of God.

The Archbishop.

Will you be faithful in Ordaining, sending, or laying hands upon others?

Answer. I will so be, by the help of God.

The Archbishop.

Will you shew yourself gentle, and be merciful, for Christ's sake, to poor and needy people, and to all strangers destitute of help?

Answer. I will so shew myself, by God's help.

Then the Archbishop, standing up, shall say,

Almighty God, our heavenly Father, who hath given you a good will to do all these things, grant also unto you strength and power to perform the same; that, he accomplishing in you the good work which he hath begun, you may be found perfect and irreprehensible at the last day, through Jesus Christ our Lord. Amen.

Then shall *Veni Creator Spiritus* be said.

Come, Holy Ghost, our Souls inspire,
And lighten with celestial fire.
Thou the anointing Spirit art,
Who dost thy sev'nfold gifts impart:
Thy blessed Unction from above,
Is comfort, life, and fire of love.
Enable with perpetual light,
The dullness of our blinded sight:
Anoint and cheer our soiled face
With the abundance of thy grace:
Keep far our foes, give peace at home;
Where thou art guide no ill can come.
Teach us to know the Father, Son,
And thee of both, to be but one:
That through the ages all along,
This may be our endless Song;
Praise to thy eternal merit,
Father, Son, and Holy Spirit.

That ended, the Superintendant shall say,

Lord, hear our prayer.

Ans. And let our cry come unto thee.

The Superintendant.

Let us pray.

Almighty God and most merciful Father, who of thine infinite goodness hast given thine only and dearly beloved Son Jesus Christ to be our Redeemer, and the Author of everlasting life, who, after that he had made perfect our redemption by his death, and was ascended into heaven, poured down his gifts abundantly upon men,

---

things; Grant also unto you strength and power to perform the same; that he accomplishing in you the good work which he hath begun, you may be found perfect and irreprehensible at the latter day; through Jesus Christ our Lord. Amen.

Then shall the Bishop elect put on the rest of the Episcopal habit; and kneeling down, *Veni Creator Spiritus*, shall be sung or said over him, the Archbishop beginning and the Bishops, with others that are present, answering by verses, as followeth..

Come, Holy Ghost, our Souls inspire,
And lighten with celestial fire.
Thou the anointing Spirit art,
Who dost thy sev'nfold gifts impart:
Thy blessed Unction from above,
Is comfort, life, and fire of love.
Enable with perpetual light,
The dullness of our blinded sight:
Anoint and cheer our soiled face
With the abundance of thy grace:
Keep far our foes, give peace at home;
Where thou art guide no ill can come.
Teach us to know the Father, Son,
And thee of both, to be but one:
That through the ages all along,
This may be our endless Song;
Praise to thy eternal merit,
Father, Son, and Holy Spirit.

Or this:

Come, Holy Ghost, eternal God, &c. [Cranmer's version]

As before in the Form for Ordering Priests.

That ended, the Archbishop shall say,

Lord, hear our prayer.

Answer. And let our cry come unto thee.

Let us pray.

Almighty God and most merciful Father, who of thine infinite goodness hast given thine only and dearly beloved Son Jesus Christ, to be our Redeemer and the Author of everlasting life; who, after that he had made perfect our redemption by his death, and was ascended into heaven, poured down his gifts abundantly upon men, making some Apostles, some Prophets, some Evangelists, some Pastors and Doctors, to the edifying and making perfect his church; grant, we beseech thee, to this thy servant such grace, that he may evermore be ready to spread abroad thy gospel, the glad tidings of reconciliation with thee, and use the authority given him, not to destruction, but to salvation; not to hurt, but to help; so that, as a wise and faithful servant, giving to thy Family their portion in due season, he may at last be received into everlasting joy, through Jesus Christ our Lord, who, with thee and the Holy Ghost, liveth and reigneth, One God, world without end, Amen.

Then the Superintendant and Elders present shall lay their Hands upon the Head of the elected Person kneeling before them upon his knees, the Superintendant saying,

Receive the Holy Ghost for the office and work of a Superintendant in the church of God, now committed unto thee by the imposition of our hands, in the Name of the Father, and of the Son, and of the Holy Ghost. Amen. And remember that thou stir up the grace of God which is given thee by this imposition of our hands; for God hath not given us the spirit of fear, but of power, and love, and soberness.

Then the Superintendant shall deliver him the Bible, saying,

Give heed unto reading, exhortation, and doctrine. Think upon these things contained in this book. Be diligent in them, that the increase coming thereby may be manifest unto all men. Take heed unto thyself, and to thy doctrine; for by so doing thou shalt both save thyself and them that hear thee. Be to the flock of Christ a shepherd, not a wolf; feed them, devour them not. Hold up the weak, heal the sick, bind up the broken, bring again the outcasts, seek the lost. Be so merciful, that you be not too remiss; so minister discipline that you forget not mercy; that when the chief shepherd shall appear, you may receive the never-fading crown of

making some Apostles, some Prophets, some Evangelists, some Pastors and Doctors, to the edifying and making perfect his Church: Grant, we beseech thee, to this thy servant such grace, that he may evermore be ready to spread abroad thy gospel, the glad tidings of reconciliation with thee; and use the authority given him, not to destruction, but to salvation; not to hurt, but to help: so that, as a wise and faithful servant, giving to thy family their portion in due season, he may at last be received into everlasting joy; through Jesus Christ our Lord, who with thee and the Holy Ghost, liveth and reigneth, One God, world without end, Amen.

Then the Archbishop and Bishops present shall lay their hands upon the head of the elected Bishop kneeling before them upon his knees, the Archbishop saying,

Receive the Holy Ghost for the office and work of a Bishop in the Church of God, now committed unto thee by the imposition of our hands; In the Name of the Father, and of the Son, and of the Holy Ghost. Amen. And remember that thou stir up the grace of God which is given thee by this imposition of our hands: for God hath not given us the spirit of fear, but of power, and love, and soberness.

Then the Archbishop shall deliver him the Bible, saying,

Give heed unto reading, exhortation, and doctrine. Think upon these things contained in this Book. Be diligent in them, that the increase coming thereby may be manifest unto all men. Take heed unto thyself, and to doctrine; for by so doing thou shalt both save thyself and them that hear thee. Be to the flock of Christ a shepherd, not a wolf; feed them, devour them not. Hold up the weak, heal the sick, bind up the broken, bring again the outcasts, seek the lost. Be so merciful, that you be not too remiss: so minister discipline that you forget not mercy: that when the chief Shepherd shall appear, ye may receive the never-fading crown of glory, through Jesus Christ our Lord. Amen.

Then the Superintendant shall proceed in the Communion Service, with whom the newly-ordained Superintendant, and other Persons present, shall communicate.

And for the last Collect, immediately before the Benediction, shall be said these Prayers.

Most merciful Father, we beseech thee to send down upon this thy servant thy heavenly blessing, and so endue him with thy Holy Spirit, that he, preaching thy word, may not only be earnest to reprove, beseech, and rebuke with all patience and doctrine, but also may be to such as believe a wholesome example in word, in conversation, in love, in faith, in chastity, and in purity; that faithfully fulfilling his course, at the latter day he may receive the crown of righteousness laid up by the Lord, the righteous Judge, who liveth and reigneth one God with the Father and the Holy Ghost, world without end. Amen.

Prevent us, O Lord, in all our doings with thy most gracious favour, and further us with thy continual help; that in all our works begun, continued, and ended in thee, we may glorify thy holy Name, and finally by thy mercy, obtain everlasting life, through Jesus Christ our Lord. Amen.

The peace of God, which passeth all understanding, keep your hearts and minds in the knowledge and love of God, and of his Son Jesus Christ our Lord. And the blessing of God almighty, the Father, the Son, and the Holy Ghost, be amongst you, and remain with you always. Amen.

glory; through Jesus Christ our Lord. Amen.

Then the Archbishop shall proceed in the Communion Service; with whom the newly consecrated Bishop (with others) shall also communicate.

And for the last Collect, immediately before the Benediction, shall be said these Prayers.

Most merciful Father, we beseech thee to send down upon this thy servant thy heavenly blessing; and so endue him with thy Holy Spirit, that he, preaching thy Word, may not only be earnest to reprove, beseech, and rebuke with all patience and doctrine; but also may be to such as believe a wholesome example, in word, in conversation, in love, in faith, in chastity, and in purity; that faithfully fulfilling his course, at the latter day he may receive the crown of righteousness laid up by the Lord the righteous Judge, who liveth and reigneth one God with the Father and the Holy Ghost, world without end. Amen.

Prevent us, O Lord, in all our doings with thy most gracious favour, and further us with thy continual help; that in all our works, begun, continued, and ended in thee, we may glorify thy holy Name, and finally by thy mercy, obtain everlasting life, through Jesus Christ our Lord. Amen.

The peace of God, which passeth all understanding, keep your hearts and minds in the knowledge and love of God, and of his Son Jesus Christ our Lord: And the blessing of God almighty, the Father, the Son, and the Holy Ghost, be amongst you, and remain with you always. Amen. [1]

---

1   The texts reproduced are from the first edition of Wesley's abridgement of the Prayer Book and an edition of the *Book of Common Prayer (1662)* which is contemporary to Wesley's time.

Epilogue

'Be Church of England Men Still'

John Wesley believed that the whole structure and development of his ministry amongst the Methodists was a necessary, although extraordinary, expedient towards the enlivening of the Church of England. He was a man possessed by the overwhelming calling to shake that church from its sloth and despondency. People were dying in ignorance of the Gospel, untouched by the ministrations of Christ's church, and John Wesley could not stand idly by. He could not wait for the Church of England to raise itself from its organisational, spiritual, and theological torpor. The people were in need and their need had to be addressed immediately.

The challenge of John Wesley's evangelistic calling required him to lay aside the shield of established authority and order, that he might move, more freely, into the hinterland of human social and spiritual deprivation. Although he did lay down that shield, he did so with great difficulty, feeling exposed and vulnerable. Conformity to the authority of prayer book rubric and Church of England canon had been so established as his raison d'être of ministry that it was difficult for him to turn away from them, but turn away from them he knew he must. So long as he accepted the rubrics and canons as governing principles, his ministry beyond the boundaries would be hindered.

John Wesley knew that, having laid aside the authority and order structures of the established church, it was essential that he replaced them with some other governing principles. If he did not do so, then the Methodist movement, which was growing around him, would soon extend beyond his control, and cease to fulfil its purpose – that being the raising up of the Church of England. The spiritual enlivenment of that church was the fruit towards which John Wesley believed himself called to work.

Behind Wesley's urgency to enliven the Church of England lay his awareness of the enormity of need to be found amongst the people of eighteenth–century England. He knew that the church was not meeting that need. He did not seek to raise up the church for its own sake, but for the sake of those who did not yet belong to it. The need for evangelisation of the unchurched masses weighed heavily upon John Wesley's mind; if the Church was not yet able to reach them then he must do it himself. Therefore, the two aspects of his purpose intertwined; the raising up of the Church of England and the bringing into faith of the unchurched people.

So it was that John Wesley understood himself to be the recipient, from God, of both an ordinary and an extraordinary calling. His ordinary calling was to be a priest in the Church of England, his extraordinary calling was to do the work of an evangelist amongst those not yet touched by the ministrations of the church. John Wesley was not on his own in this calling but was one of a group of similarly minded clergymen in the Church of England. Men such as his brother Charles Wesley, his close associate George Whitefield, his friends Grimshaw of Haworth, Venn of Huddersfield, Walker of Truro, worked together with John Wesley.

John Wesley's significance lay in his freedom to travel and his organisational ability. Being a Fellow of an Oxford College, John Wesley was not tied to a particular parish, but was free to exercise his ministry throughout England. The same could presumably be said of his brother Charles. Similarly, George Whitefield seems to have been constant in his work as an itinerant evangelist. John Wesley differed from both these men, however, in that he had the flair for working-out structures and organisations. Whitefield was the great orator, Charles Wesley the great poet and hymn-writer – they appeared to have neither time nor concern for the structures of organisation that seemed to be so fascinating to John Wesley and essential to his movement.

John Wesley's development of the structures and organisations of Methodism was partly the result of, and partly the cause of, his need to maintain authority and order amongst those who came to Christianity through his work. In the absence of satisfactory spiritual oversight from the established church, John Wesley felt it necessary that he should exercise the care and direction of those associated with him. So it was that Wesley's understanding of being the scriptural *episcopos* of the people called Methodists came about.

As John Wesley's ministry developed, as the results of his travelling became more substantial, as the number of Methodist societies grew, so it became more difficult for him to exercise the necessary control and oversight of his people. So Wesley allowed the development of the ministry of local leaders as his Assistants, to give him help in the care of his societies. The network of lay leaders, stewards, class leaders, Assistants and preachers grew around the Methodist societies, drawing into positions of leadership many who were regarded by critics as totally unworthy and unsuited to the task. Wesley, though, tested the ministry of those associated with him according to its fruit; if the development was of God then it would live to bear fruit.

John Wesley never lost sight of his understanding of God's purpose in raising up the Methodist people. The purpose was not the founding of a new church community, but the enlivenment of the established Church of England. He claimed, always, to being faithful to the church of his ordination, rejecting all suggestions that he was moving beyond her fellowship. If he did find himself beyond the boundaries of the established church, then it was only because that church had drawn its boundaries in the wrong place. He recognised that there were a group of people who were on the margins of society and church, in his reaching out to them he realised that he was reaching over the established borders of convention. He did so willingly, believing himself called so to do. He did so purposefully, believing himself setting the good example for what he believed the church as a whole should be doing.

So it was, when discussing the purpose of his having established a body of Methodist preachers, John Wesley stated that they were to be regarded as extraordinary messengers. They were a temporary work force, not a permanent ministry. The intention was that the extraordinary messengers were to provoke the ordinary messengers, the ministers of the Church of England, to jealousy. He regarded the preachers as a necessary expedient in the work of raising up and enlivening the Church of England. Once that church had been raised up and enlivened, he envisaged that his work force would no longer be needed and so could be disbanded, or brought into the regular ministry of orders in the Church of England.

It was necessary that John Wesley maintain a strict control upon the Methodist societies. Having read the work of King and Stillingfleet, John Wesley became clear in his mind that it was quite acceptable for him to exercise spiritual oversight of the Methodist people. He regarded himself as the scriptural *episcopos* of the body of people who had come together through his ministry. He regarded himself as having the responsibility to care for his people, until the Church of England was in a position to take them over. Consequently he regarded himself as fulfilling the episcopal function, governing their lives, directing their ministries, and exercising discipline over them.

John Wesley exercised his authority and control over the Methodist people with great vigour and little apparent flexibility. He had always exercised authority in this manner – what had changed was the source and nature of that authority. In the early years of his ministry his pastoral authority had been established in terms of prayer book rubric and canon law. After his Aldersgate experience John Wesley was increasingly guided, in his exercise of authority, by the demands of his extraordinary and evangelistic calling. To some, he might appear as an idiosyncratic despot, but he was a man driven by a vision and hounded by responsibility. His salvation depended upon his fidelity to the call of God. This call had charged him with the care of many souls who, without the care of the church, would be forever lost into the flaming pit of ignorance. He regarded himself to be the guardian of the souls of those who joined him, until such time as he could introduce them into a Church of England into which the Spirit of God had blown life.

To John Wesley's great consternation, he became aware that there were many who sought the cutting loose of Methodism from the Church of England. He could not allow such an action, for it had never been his intention to create a body of Christians separate from the established church. The arguments of his people, though, were strong and convincing. The ministers of the established church were frequently rejecting the Methodists, turning them away from their services, so depriving them of opportunity to partake of the sacraments. Some clergymen were not turning the Methodists away, but the people themselves were reluctant to avail themselves of their ministrations, believing them to be 'unsaved' and so unworthy of their calling and vocation.

The call of the Methodist people to receive the sacraments from the hands of their own preachers was becoming increasingly strong. John Wesley remained convinced that the only proper means for authorising his preachers to administer the sacraments would be for them to be ordained by prayer and the imposition of hands. At this early stage, believing that such a move would be an unacceptable breach of Church of England discipline, he resisted the demands of his people and sought to find sympathetic clergymen who were acceptable to his people to perform the sacramental ministry for them.

Many of the developments of ministry amongst the Methodists were brought about by John Wesley having to react to the actions of his people in ways which he would not have otherwise have taken. When some of his preachers had themselves licensed as dissenters, in the early 1750s, Wesley's hand was forced, and he responded by seeking episcopal ordination for some of his nominated preachers, such as Thomas Maxfield and Samuel Furly. Even at this point John Wesley did not regard his ordination of the Methodist preachers as being an option. He continuously stated that to do so would be to separate from the established church, an action which he declared to be unlawful.

When, in 1784, John Wesley was confronted with the needs of the Methodist people in the newly independent America, his first reaction was to attempt to secure a resolution by recourse to the practices of the Church of England. The lack of ordained clergymen in the new country was causing the people to be deprived of the sacraments of the church. Both John Wesley and a body of American Anglicans sought to remedy the situation in what had until then been the normal manner. They appealed to the Church of England, through the bishop of London, who had been responsible for the colonies, asking for the provision of ministers for America. The law of England made it impossible for the English bishops to ordain clergymen for America, the canons and rubrics required the swearing of an oath concerning the Royal Supremacy.

A group of American Methodist preachers decided to take matters upon themselves and administered presbyteral ordination to one another. John Wesley realised that he had to take action or else American Methodism would be lost to him. Whilst the American Anglicans turned to the Scottish bishops to ordain and consecrate Samuel Seabury, John Wesley turned to a more creative resolution. He had already been convinced by his reading of King and Stillingfleet that he was performing an episcopal function in his governing of the Methodist societies. His scruples against ordaining the preachers could not be applied to the American situation, the established church having refused to accept any jurisdiction for the former colony. He believed that the spiritual deprivation being suffered by the people required him to take action. The action he chose was the ordination of Vasey and Whatcoat, as elders, and the consecration of Thomas Coke as Superintendant. He, the scriptural episcopos of the people called Methodists, ordained Vasey, Whatcoat and Coke as Methodist preachers, not to any form of Anglican orders.

In ordaining his preachers for America, and especially in his consecration of Coke as Superintendant, John Wesley was establishing a new church in a new country. He supplied that church with a ministry, a liturgy and a doctrinal statement, all of which represented a modification of that of the Church of England. In doing so he affirmed his intention that American Methodism should practice an episcopalian polity. John Wesley did not reject the episcopalian model of church government, but affirmed it in his provision for America. It is completely wrong for any to claim that John Wesley had adopted a presbyterian polity. He was quite clearly exercising an episcopal function in relation to the Methodist preachers. The fact that, as a presbyter in the Church of England, John Wesley had absolutely no right to ordain anyone is in fact irrelevant. He believed himself to be acting as the scriptural *episcopos* of the people called Methodists, not as an Anglican presbyter. He was ordaining Methodist preachers, not Anglican presbyters, an action which he had convinced himself was within the bounds of his extraordinary authority.

John Wesley's justification for ordaining preachers for work in Scotland and the mission field was based upon arguments similar to those for his ordinations for America. He claimed that because those places were beyond the jurisdiction of the Church of England, he was not breaking with discipline. No matter how tenuous that argument, and it was very tenuous, John Wesley could in no manner justify his ordination in August 1788 of Alexander Mather as Methodist preacher to work in England.

It is possible to argue, in justification of Wesley's action, that just as he may have felt his hand being forced in America, so it was being forced in England. The preachers whom he had ordained for work in America, Scotland, and the mission field were supposed, upon return to the English work, to revert to their previous status. However, some of the preachers rebelled and, responding to the needs of their people, initiated a sacramental ministry amongst the Methodist societies under their care. Other preachers, who had not previously been ordained, began to join in the work, taking upon themselves a sacramental ministry. The situation looked as if it would get out of hand and John Wesley would lose control of his connexion.

Earlier in 1788 Charles Wesley had died and thus the most potent power against John Wesley's ordination of his preachers had been defused. It is possible that, even if the demise of brother Charles had not come at this point, John Wesley would have begun to ordain his preachers for England anyway. Having endured the continued criticism for the ordinations already performed, having borne the persistent comments about his apparent lack of will in chastising recalcitrant preachers who were taking sacramental ministry upon themselves, it would, perhaps, have been inevitable that John Wesley's patience would expire and he would have ordained his preachers. Yet, of course, he would ordain them as the Methodist *episcopos* appointing Methodist preachers to a sacramental ministry, not Anglican presbyter ordaining other presbyters. His understanding of ordination was limited to its function as the means of conveying a ministerial commission, not the giving of grace. He regarded himself as performing an act of authorisation, granting permission to his preachers to take up the sacramental ministry.

John Wesley never stopped claiming fidelity to the Church of England; he always he believed his work as being towards the revitalization of that church. Even after his English ordinations he maintained his premise that he did not anticipate that the Methodist Societies would separate from the Church of England. His sermon, referred to in this work as *Prophets and Priests*, and his dealing with the Irish preachers in 1789, show John Wesley continuing to claim his intention that the Methodist preachers were preachers only. Although accepting that, in certain circumstances, he had found it necessary to ordain some of those preachers, in order to alleviate spiritual deprivation, he rejected any suggestion that his intention for his preachers had changed. Their usual position was to be as preachers only, extraordinary messengers, not priests exercising a sacramental ministry. Furthermore, in his dealing with the difficult Irish preachers, John Wesley asserted his authority; he was still to be regarded as the scriptural episcopos, the preachers were to look to him for direction. Their ministry depended upon him alone for its course, he alone would appoint them to their work. That work was still to be regarded as the work of those who were first counted as Mr Wesley's preachers, the work of bringing light to the dark places of church and society. Even at this late stage in his life, John Wesley regarded his preachers as an extraordinary, and temporary, work force who were designed to provoke the ordinary ministers of the Church of England into life. He called them to remain faithful to that church:

> Ye yourselves were at first called in the Church of England; and though ye have and will have a thousand temptations to leave it, and set up for yourselves, regard them not; be Church of England men still; do not cast away the peculiar glory which God hath put upon you, and frustrate the design of providence, the very end for which God raised you up.[1]

---

1   Albert C. Outler (ed.), *Works*, 4: 82.

Bibliography

Baker, Frank. 'Wesley's Ordinations', in *Proceedings*, Wesley Historical Society, 24(1943).

Baker, Frank. *William Grimshaw, 1708–63.* (London: Epworth, 1963).

Baker, Frank. *John Wesley and the Church of England.* (London: Epworth, 1970)

Baker, Frank. (ed.), *Letters* 2 vols in *The Works of John Wesley,* (Nashville:Abingdon, 1987).

Benyon, Tom. (ed.) *Howell Harris, Reformer and Soldier.* (Caernarfon: Calvinistic Methodist Bookroom, 1958).

Bettenson, Henry (ed.), *Documents of the Christian Church.* (Oxford: OUP, 2nd edn, 1963).

Bowmer, John C. and Vickers, John A. (eds), *The Letters of John Pawson (Methodist Itinerant, 1762–1806).* 3 vols. (Peterborough: Methodist Publishing House).

Bowmer, John C. 'Ordinations in Methodism 1791–1836'. in *Proceedings*, Wesley Historical Society, 36(1967–8).

Campbell, Dennis M. *The Yoke of Obedience: The Meaning of Ordination in Methodism.* (Nashville: Abingdon, 1988).

Campbell, Ted A. *John Wesley and Christian Antiquity.* (Nashville: Kingswood, 1991).

Campbell, Ted A. *The Religion of the Heart: A Study of European Religious life in the Seventeenth and Eighteenth Centuries.* (Columbia: University of South Carolina, 1991).

Chilcote, Paul W. *John Wesley and the Women preachers of Early Methodism.* (Metuchen, N.J.: Scarecrow Press, 1991).

Chilcote, Paul W. *She Offered them Christ: The Legacy of Women Preachers in Early Methodism.* (Nashville: Abingdon, 1993).

Chilcote, Paul W. *Recapturing the Wesley's Vision.* (Illinois: IVP, 2004).

Clark, Elmer T., Potts, J. Manning and Payton, Jacob S. (eds.), *The Journal and Letters of Francis Asbury.* 3 vols. (Nashville: Abingdon, 1958).

Coke, Thomas and Moore, Henry. *The Life of the Rev John Wesley, A.M.,* (London: Paramore, 1792).

Collins, Kenneth J. *John Wesley: A Theological Journey.* (Nashville: Abingdon, 2003).

Cragg, Gerald R. (ed.), *The Appeals to Men of Reason and Religion and Certain Open Letters,* in *The Works of John Wesley.* (Oxford: Clarendon, 1975).

Curnock, Nehemiah (ed.), *The Journal of the Rev John Wesley, A.M.,* 8 vols. (London: Robert Culley, 1909-16).

Dallimore, A.A. *George Whitefield.* 2 vols. Edinburgh: Banner of Truth).

Davies, R., George, A. Raymond, Rupp, E. Gordon. (eds.), *A History of the Methodist Church in Great Britain.* 4 vols. (London: Epworth, 1965–88).

Downey, James. *The Eighteenth Century Pulpit.* (Oxford: Clarendon, 1969).

Etheridge, J.W., *The Life of the Rev Adam Clark.* (London: John Mason, 1858).

Etheridge, J.W. *The Life of the Rev Thomas Coke, D.C.L.*
     (London: John Mason, 1860).

Evans, G.R. and Wright, J. Robert (eds.), *The Anglican Tradition*
     (London:SPCK/Minneapolis: Fortress, 1991).

Gregory, Benjamin. *Sidelights on the Conflicts of Methodism, 1827–52.*
     (London: Caswell, 1899).

Gunter, W. Stephen. *The Limits of 'Love Divine'.* (Nashville: Kingswood, 1989).

Heitzenrater, Richard P. *Mirror and Memory: Reflections on Early Methodism.*
     (Nashville: Kingswood, 1989).

Heitzenrater, Richard P. *Wesley and the People Called Methodists.*
     (Nashville: Abingdon, 1995).

Heitzenrater, Richard P. *The Elusive Mr Wesley.* Second Edition.
     (Nashville: Abingdon, 2003).

Henry, Stuart. *George Whitefield: Wayfaring Witness.*
     (Nashville: Abingdon, 1957).

Hilderbrandt, Franz and Beckerlegge, Oliver A. (eds), *A Collection of Hymns for
     the Use of People called Methodists,* in *The Works of John Wesley.*
     (Nashville: Abingdon, 1983).

Hunter, Frederick. *Sources of Wesley's Revisions of the Prayer Book 1784–8,* in
     Proceedings, Wesley Historical Society, 23(1941–2).

Jackson, Thomas. (ed.) *The Works of the Rev John Wesley, A.M.* 14 vols.
     (London: John Mason, 1829-31).

Jackson, Thomas. *Lives of the Early Methodist Preachers,* 6 vols.
     (London: John Mason, 1837-38).

Jackson, Thomas. *Life of Charles Wesley, A.M.* 2 vols.
     (London: John Mason, 1841).

Jasper, R.C.D. *The Development of the Anglican Liturgy 1662–1980.*
     (London: SPCK, 1989).

Kimbrough, S.T. and Beckerlegge, Oliver A. (eds). *The Unpublished Poetry of
     Charles Wesley,* 3 vols. (Nashville: Kingswood, 1992).

King, Peter. *An Enquiry into the Constitution, Discipline, Unity and Worship of the
     Primitive Church,* (London: n.p., 1691).

Kirby, James E. *The Episcopacy in American Methodism.*
     (Nashville: Kingswood, 2000).

Kirby, James E., Richey, Russell E. and Rowe, Kenneth E. *The Methodists.*
     (Connecticut: Greenwood Press, 1996)

Klaiber, Walter and Marquardt, Manfred. *Living Grace: An Outline of United
     Methodist Theology.* (Nashville: Abingdon, 2001).

Lacey, H. Edward, *John Wesley's Ordinations,* in *Proceedings,* Wesley Historical
     Society, 33 (1961).

Lawson, A.B. *John Wesley and the Christian Ministry: The Sources and
     Development of his Opinions and Practice.* (London: SPCK, 1963).

Lyles, A.M. *Methodism Mocked: The Satiric Reaction to Methodism in the
     Eighteenth Century,* (London: Epworth, 1960).

　　　　　　　　　　　　Authority and Order

Maddox, Randy L. (ed.), *Rethinking Wesley's Theology for Contemporary Methodism*. (Nashville: Kingswood, 1998).

Monk, Robert C. *John Wesley: His Puritan Heritage*, (London: Epworth, 1966).

Moore, Henry. *The Life of the Rev John Wesley, A.M.* 2 vols. (London: John Kershaw, 1825).

Newton, John A. *Susanna Wesley and the Puritan Tradition in Methodism*. (Peterborough: Epworth, 2002).

Outler, Albert C. *John Wesley*. (Oxford: OUP, 1964).

Outler, Albert C. 'The Ordinal' in Dunkie and Quillan (eds)*, Companion to the Book of Worship*, (Nashville: Abingdon, 1970).

Outler, Albert C. (ed.), *Sermons*, in *The Works of John Wesley*, (Nashville: Abingdon, 1987).

Peaston, A.E. *The Prayer Book Tradition in the Free Churches*, (London: James Clarke & Co., 1964).

Rack, Henry. *Reasonable Enthusiast*. (London: Epworth, 1989).

Richey, Russell E. *The Methodist Conference in America: A History*. (Nashville: Kingswood, 1996).

Rupp, E. Gordon. *Religion in England 1688–1791*, (Oxford: OUP, 1986).

Sackett, A.B. *John Wesley and the Greek Orthodox Bishop*, in *Proceedings*, Wesley Historical Society, 38 (1972).

Simon, J.S. 'Wesley's Ordinations', in *Proceedings*, Wesley Historical Society, 9(1913-14).

Smith, Haddon. *Methodistical Deceit: A Sermon Preached in the Parish Church of St Matthew, Bethnal Green, Middlesex*. (London: H. Turpin, 1770).

Stillingfleet, Edward. *Irenicum*, (London: n.p., 1661).

Telford, John. *Wesley Veterans: Lives of the Early Methodist Preachers*, 7 vols. (London: Epworth, 1912–4).

Telford, John (ed.), *The Letters of the Rev John Wesley, A.M.* 8 vols. (London: Epworth, 1931).

Thompson, Edgar W. *Wesley: Apostolic Man, Some Reflections on Wesley's Consecration of Dr Thomas Coke*. (London: Epworth, 1957).

Turner, John Munsey. *John Wesley: The Evangelical Revival and the Rise of Methodism in England*. (Peterborough: Epworth Press, 2002).

Tyerman, Luke. *Life and Times of John Wesley*, 3 vols. (London: Hodder and Stoughton, 1870-71).

Ward, W. Reginald and Heitzenrater, Richard P. (eds), *Journals and Diaries,* in *The Works of John Wesley*, (Nashville: Abingdon, 1988.

Ward, W. Reginald. *Faith and Faction*. (London: Epworth Press, 1993).

Ware, Thomas. *Sketches of the Life and Travels of Thomas Ware*, (New York: T. Mason and G. Lane, 1832).

Watson, David Lowes. *Class Leaders: Recovering a Tradition*. (Nashville: Discipleship Resources, 1991).

Watson, David Lowes. *The Early Methodist Class Meeting: Its Origin and Significance.* (Nashville: Discipleship Resources, 1985).

Watson, Richard. *The Life of John Wesley*, (London: John Mason, 1831).

White, James F. *John Wesley's Prayer Book: The Sunday Service of the Methodists in North America*, (Cleveland: Order of St. Luke, 1991).

Williams, Colin. *John Wesley's Theology Today*, (London: Epworth, 1960).

Index

.

For Product Safety Concerns and Information please contact our EU
representative GPSR@taylorandfrancis.com
Taylor & Francis Verlag GmbH, Kaufingerstraße 24, 80331 München, Germany

www.ingramcontent.com/pod-product-compliance
Lightning Source LLC
Chambersburg PA
CBHW060348100426
42812CB00003B/1170

9 780754 654544